GREAT DISASTERS
OF THE STAGE

. . . handed the stage-door keys to the leading man . . .

GREAT DISASTERS OF THE STAGE

William Donaldson

Illustrated by Bernard Cookson

Arthur Barker Limited   London
A subsidiary of Weidenfeld (Publishers) Limited

ALSO BY WILLIAM DONALDSON

Both the Ladies and the Gentlemen
Letters to Emma Jane
The Balloons in the Black Bag
The Henry Root Letters
The Further Letters of Henry Root
Henry Root's World of Knowledge
The English Way of Doing Things

Published in Great Britain by
Arthur Barker Limited
91 Clapham High Street
London SW4 7TA

ISBN 0 213 16908 8

Printed in Great Britain by
Redwood Burn Limited,
Trowbridge, Wiltshire

Contents

Acknowledgements

I cannot adequately express my gratitude to Jenny Prior, an incomparable researcher, who must have ploughed through a hundred chortling theatrical memoirs and yet remained cheerful, more or less. She would want me to say, however, that any errors, exaggerations, sillinesses or downright libels that may have crept in hereunder are due to her.

Obviously I can guarantee the truth only of those stories that have to do with my own efforts to mount plays. With money left to me by my father, honourably acquired by him shipping this and that to Canada from Glasgow, I went into theatrical management in 1958 with a colossal flop by Hubert 'Maybe It's Because I'm a Londoner' Gregg and was involuntarily liquidated twelve years later after a fiasco called *Council Of Love*. Between them, apart from two errors of judgement, was a series of grotesque blunders. The errors of judgement were *Beyond The Fringe* and *The Premise*. The former fell into my lap after its triumph at the 1960 Edinburgh Festival because its creators judged that I was the only impresario in London too wet and inexperienced to insist on the addition of scenery, an orchestra, dancing girls and Kenneth Williams for its West End run. I produced *The Premise* entirely by mistake. For reasons that must have seemed sound at the time, I asked Arthur Johnston, who had been captain of boxing at Winchester but was currently an estate agent, I think, to book *The Second City*, an exceptionally clever improvisational group from Chicago. He booked *The Premise*, I don't know why, who traded in New York and did the same sort of thing, though much less skilfully. No one was more surprised than I when the curtain went up on *The Premise*, unless it was the keen PR lady who for a month had been alerting London to the arrival of *The Second City*.

It is too late, alas, to apologise to the many serious people harmed by my silly antics, but I wouldn't want to seem boastful about these flops. It may seem funny now to think of Moira Lister (or Vicomtesse d'Orthez, as she then was and no doubt still is) being knocked as flat as a pancake by a piece of faulty scenery, and it was jolly funny at the time too, though not to her I imagine, nor to the scenery builder who almost certainly hadn't been paid.

What seem to me the amusing bits in this book have been lifted as clean as a whistle and without so much as a by your leave from Christopher Logue's marvellous *True Stories* (Private Eye/Andre Deutsch £2.75 and a steal at the price). None of them has much to do with the theatre, but they are all the better for that in my opinion, so there you are.

W.D.

Bad Audiences

Indignant spectators who spat at Noël Coward after the first night of *Sirocco* in 1927, obliging the Master to send his dress-coat to the cleaners, and their successors, who, enraged by the play's ambitious theme and the arrival on-stage almost immediately of a German philosopher, actually began to boo Peter Ustinov's *No Sign Of The Dove* just forty-five seconds after the curtain had gone up, were merely following a time-honoured tradition of audience hooliganism dating back to 1660. Theatres at that time had been dark for eighteen years, closed by order of Mrs Whitehouse's seventeenth-century representatives, and when they reopened, audiences, released at last from the straightjacket of puritanism were naturally a little boisterous, liking to pelt actors who had displeased them with missiles and abuse, and, when bored, mounting alternative entertainments in the stalls.

One contemporary report reads: 'On Thursday night there was a great riot at Covent Garden, without the least plea or pretence whatever, occasioned by the gentry in the upper gallery calling for a hornpipe, though nothing of the sort was expressed in the bills. Then a Mr Goodyear and a Mr Fielding – who had bought highly priced seats near the stage – drew their swords and engaged in a duel while the play was going on. An orange was thrown at Mr Sheridan, who was playing the character of Aesop, and so well directed that it dented the iron of his false nose and drove it into his head.'

Throughout the eighteenth and early nineteenth centuries, even the most celebrated and popular performers were considered fair game for target practice. The supporters of one star – Kean or Kemble, say – would, for a lively night on the town, visit a theatre where another star – David Garrick, for instance – was appearing, merely to cause trouble. Like the football hooligans of today, however, they were rigidly conservative. In their view there were traditional ways to play Shakespeare and traditional ways of dressing for a part. On one occasion Garrick tried to suggest Macbeth's inner turmoil by leaving the buttons of his waistcoat undone. The audience, flabbergasted by this departure from tradition, threw eggs and tomatoes at him, forcing him to leave the stage.

To avoid rowdyism of this sort, actors and playwrights packed the theatres with their own supporters, leaving little room for trouble-makers: a system thought to be foolproof until Charles Lamb, having filled Drury Lane with his friends for the first night of his play *Mr H*, surprised everyone by leading the booing himself. After a matter of minutes he decided that he couldn't tolerate the work, which purported to be a farce. Its only joke consisted in the leading character being called 'Hogflesh', after a famous cricketer. Judging this to be particularly feeble in performance, Lamb jumped up and down on his hat and cried, 'An outrage! A nausea! Ring down the curtain, I say!'

Some contemporary theatre-lovers regretted that plays couldn't be performed without riots and disorders. In 1749, a Mr W.R.Chetwood wrote:

'I remember about twenty years past, I was one of the audience at a new play. Before me sat a sea-officer with whom I had some acquaintance; on each hand of him disported a couple of sparks, both prepared with their offensive instruments vulgarly termed cat-calls, which they were tuning up before the play began.

'The officer did not take any notice of them till the curtain drew up; but when they continued their sow-gelder's music he begged they would not prevent his hearing the actors, tho' *they* might not care whether they heard or no; but they took little notice of his civil request, which he repeated again and again to no purpose. But at last one of them condescended to tell him that if he did not like it, he might leave it alone.

'"Why really," replied the sea-captain. "I do not like it,

and would have *you* let your noise alone. I have paid my money to see and hear the play, and your ridiculous noise not only hinders me, but a great many other people that are here, I believe, with the same design. Now, if you prevent us, you rob us of our money and our time ; therefore I beg you, as you look like a gentleman, to behave as such."

'One of them seemed mollified and put his whistle in his pocket, but the other was incorrigible. The blunt sea-captain made him one speech more.

'"Sir," said he. "I advise you once more to follow the example of this gentleman, and put up your pipe."

'But the piper sneered in his face and clapped the trouble-some instrument to his mouth, with cheeks swelled out like a trumpeter to give it a redoubled and louder noise ; but, like the broken crow of a cock in a fright, the squeak was stopt in the middle by a blow from the officer which he gave him with so strong a will that his child's trumpet was struck thro' his cheek and his companion led him to a surgeon.'

Standards of dress too were a cause of protest, the desirability of admitting chimney-sweeps in their working-clothes being much debated. William Ellaston, the actor-manager of the Surrey Theatre, received this letter in 1825 :

'Sir, I have with my wife been much in the habit of visiting the Surrey Theatre and on three occasions we have been annoyed by sweeps. People will not go, sir, where sweeps are; and you will find, sooner or later, these gentle-men will have the whole theatre to themselves, unless an alteration be made. I own, at some theatres, managers are too particular in dress ; those days are past, and the public have a right to go to theatrical entertainments in their morning costumes ; but this ought not to include the sweeps. It is not a week ago since my wife in a nice white gown sat down on the very spot which a sweep had just quitted, and, when she got up, the sight was most horrible, for she is a heavy lady and had laughed a good deal during the performance, but it was no laughing matter when she got home.'

One customer who thought managements were too particular on points of dress wrote to John Ebers, lessee of the King's Theatre, in the Haymarket, in 1828. Ebers recorded in his autobiography:

'I received a specimen of an epistle from a gentleman who, having presented himself for admission at the pit-door, in a pair of drab pantaloons, was, in accordance with a well-known and approved regulation, refused entrance as not being in dress. He was astonished at this. "For," says his letter, "I was dressed in a superfine blue coat with gold buttons, a white waistcoat, fashionable tight drab pantaloons, white silk stockings, and dress shoes. All worn but once, a few days before at a dress concert at the Crown And Tavern."

'He proceeds to express his indignation at the idea of the manager presuming to enact presumptory laws without the intervention of the legislature, with threats of legal proceedings and an appeal to a British jury. "I have mixed too much in genteel society," he continues, "not to know that black breeches, or pantaloons, with black silk stockings, is a very prevailing full dress; and why is it so? Because it is convenient and economical. For you can wear a pair of white silk stockings but once without washing, and a pair of black is frequently worn for weeks without ablution. P.S. I have no objection to submit an inspection of my dress of the evening in question to you or any competent person you may choose to appoint."'

In more recent times, Tallulah Bankhead solved a similar problem with greater aplomb. Told that she couldn't watch the cabaret at the Café de Paris because she was wearing trousers, she simply removed them and proceeded to her table by the stage, parrying on the way a fulsome approach by old Bendor Westminster, who hadn't seen her for ten years, with a withering 'I thought I told you to wait in the car?'

. . . when she got up, the sight was most horrible . . .

Though modern audiences seldom throw vegetables at the cast or indulge in duels on stage, they can still express their displeasure vigorously when an entertainment falls short of their expectations. The aforementioned *Sirocco* by Noël Coward, with Ivor Novello and Frances Doble, was certainly such a piece. When Ivor Novello presented himself in blue silk pyjamas in Act I, the customers decided they had never seen anything funnier. When he became passionate in Act II, they yelled and hooted, and when he kissed Miss Doble they shrieked with laughter and punctuated his lines with grunts and animal noises. Miss Doble was so confused that when someone shouted from the gallery, 'Give the old cow a chance!' she replied, 'Thank you sir, you're the only gentleman here.' At the final curtain, the stage management mistook the bedlam of abuse for enthusiasm and for a full seven minutes raised and lowered the curtain on the humiliated cast. When the hubbub subsided a little, Francis Doble, shocked out of her wits, surprised everyone by stepping forward and making her prepared curtain speech. 'Ladies and gentlemen,' she said, 'thank you for making this the happiest night of my life.'

Early in his career, Sir John Gielgud did Shakespearean recitations on a music-hall bill. It was his misfortune to be sandwiched between the seals and a twenty-stone xylophone player, Teddy 'Jazzer' Brown, both popular turns. When Sir John appeared in tights as the lovelorn Romeo there were indignant cries each night of 'Get her off! Bring back the seals! We want Jazzer Brown!'

John Bird claims that in his youth he was present when Sir Donald Wolfit did *Othello* in Nottingham. At the end of the performance, Sir Donald Stepped forward to make his curtain speech.

'Next week we shall be doing *Hamlet*,' he said. 'I myself will take the part of the irresolute Dane and my wife, Rosalind Iden, will play Ophelia.'

There was an incredulous protest from the gallery. 'Your wife's a ratbag!'

Sir Donald considered the point. 'Nevertheless,' he said at last, 'she will be appearing as Ophelia.'

Playing Richard III in 1962, Paul Daneman stopped the show after thirty minutes because six Henrys in paper hats and false noses were shouting jokes at him from a box. Unless they stopped, he said, he would leave the stage. They didn't, so Mr Daneman went home.

Jamie Rutherford, a 25-year-old insurance broker, admitted afterwards that he had been the ringleader. 'I have no intention of apologizing to Mr Daneman,' he said. 'I think we were funnier than he was.'

Arthur Marshall recalls attending a longish play, written for two characters only, a husband and wife. The scene was their living-room; the plot, such as it was, their everyday lives. Nothing much happened and the audience dozed off. Suddenly in the third act there was a sharp ring at the front-door. 'Whoever can that be?' said the wife, upon which a desperate voice from the stalls shouted, 'Let them in, whoever they are.'

In 1963 Joyce Grenfell took her evening of drawing-room recitations to Sydney, Australia. Her pianist tinkled out a harmless intro and Joyce steadied herself to open with a Flanders and Swann ditty about gnus. 'Stick it up the poms!' shouted a man in the gallery, a proposal keenly seconded in other parts of the house. Joyce returned to England to play arch musical guessing games on BBC2.

In 1976 a riot of angry Scottish migrants cut short a Billy Connolly concert in Brisbane.

The Scots, reasonably expecting a younger version of Andy Stewart, were enraged by the yellow-wellied Big Yin's unintelligible jokes. After his first number they stormed the stage, demanding their money back. One kilted loon grabbed the microphone and made a speech; another seized Connolly's guitar and smashed it to the floor; a third, a twenty-stone giant, thought to be a police inspector, collared tour manager Ian Smith, wrestled him upside down and bounced his head against the stage as though malleting a croquet hoop.

Connolly curled up like a hedgehog and pretended to be dead. 'They'd have killed me otherwise,' he said later.

In 1978 there was a full house at the Barmara Theatre near Adelaide for a performance of the award-winning play, *The Bard's Banquet*, sponsored by the Arts Council of South Australia. The play was set at the Mermaid Tavern and the action consisted of Shakespeare, Jonson and Marlowe eating a meal on stage, singing popular songs of the day and telling stories about their lives. Because the food for the cast was late arriving at the theatre, the curtain didn't go up until ten-thirty, by which time the audience, who hadn't eaten, were almost delirious with hunger.

'As the actors consumed their first course – potted shrimps – several people of both sexes began to shout out that the food should be shared between cast and audience,' said Mr Robin Williams, the house manager. 'And when Mr Bee (who was playing Shakespeare) appealed for order he was pelted with beer-cans. By the time the ox was brought on, the audience had lost control. A man jumped on to the stage and threw portions of the ox into the auditorium. Then some of the crowd occupied the stage, threw the actors into the stalls and fought hand-to-hand battles with each other over small portions of bread. One couple, shouting "We don't care! We don't care!", removed their clothes and made love in the middle of the stage; and as the police had to drive fifty miles to reach the

8

scene, nobody stopped them.'

Mr John Voysey, an official of the Arts Council of South Australia, said, 'It was a nightmare happening before my eyes. These people do not know what art is. I think Barmara should be bombed flat.'

When, in March 1984, Val Doonican tried to sing on top of Ayers Rock in Australia's Northern Territory, aborigines greased the feet of the old crooner's rocking-chair with dingo flop and gave him a gentle push. He slalomed to the bottom and, though he escaped injury, the concert was cancelled.

In December 1965 Mother Goose was shot in the foot by a pellet from an air-gun during a pantomime performance at the King's Theatre, Southsea. Dick Emery, as Simple Simon, told the audience that the show would not go on unless the shooting stopped. 'Thank you for your co-operation,' he said, and was shot in the shoulder. Police were called when two more members of the cast were also hit.

In 1974, it took a hundred *carabineri*, armed with machine-guns and smoke bombs, over four hours to subdue angry spectators at a theatre in Cantanzaro, Italy. Advance publicity for a show called *Porno-Erotico* had led the audience to expect a lively evening. The company, however, had received warning of Cantanzaro's formidable public prosecutor, Dr Massimo Bartolomei – a ferocious enemy of nudity who had already closed down six theatres and sequestered eleven films in his eight months in office. When, instead of their usual explicit convolutions, the cast juggled oranges and sang Neapolitan love songs, the audience of five hundred local businessmen tore up the seats and barricaded themselves inside the theatre. They were eventually smoked out and clubbed like farmyard rats by Dr Bartolomei and his men.

According to the *News Of The World*, all hell broke loose when the men who taught the world how to march went over the top at Brinkley's Theatre-Restaurant in Chelsea's fashionable Hollywood Road. The first fusillade of chocolate puddings flew through the air the instant the lights were dimmed and blonde stripper, Caroline Dalla, took the stage.

'It's always chocolate puddings with the Guards,' said Caroline, a leggy 25-year-old mother of two, who combines fire-eating with her strip routine. 'They wouldn't dream of trying to touch you up, but they're very keen on plastering everyone in sight with chocolate puddings. At the last show a real Henry came up to me and said, "I was supposed to be getting married at the Holy Trinity, Brompton, tomorrow, but after seeing you that's all orf. As soon as I saw you I knew you were the girl for me." Then he threw another chocolate pudding at me.'

'It takes a lot of bottle to stand up in front of 350 women and do the business,' said Johnny Flash – real name John James – a 27-year-old cockney, who has been a stripper for six years.

Mr James was speaking to reporters from a hospital bed in Doncaster after an accident the night before at Rigsby's Theatre Club on the outskirts of the grey industrial Yorkshire town.

'Strange things always happen in Doncaster,' he said. 'I'm here now because an old dear ran on-stage during the climax of my act and, grabbing my main attraction, dragged me twenty feet across the stage. Luckily it's insured !'

In April 1962, the owner of a carpet shop in Ilford opened a restaurant above the store. He called it 'The Room At The Top' and, hoping to cash in on the emerging satire boom, asked me to mount a suitable cabaret. For reasons that must have seemed sound at the time, but which now appear merely whimsical, I engaged John Wells, William Rushton and Richard Ingrams to perform the opening show. Taxed unendurably by the giggling public school humour and sub-standard Macmillan impressions, the angry diners burned the place to the ground.

Children are accomplished spell-breakers, offering blunt comments from the stalls. In 1923 Gladys Cooper played Peter Pan, the boy who wouldn't grow up. When Wendy asked Peter how old he was, a youthful voice said: 'About forty-five, I'd say.'

When Tom O'Connor, TV's Mr Clean, appeared in *Dick Whittington* he was interrupted during the always popular 'It's behind you !' routine. As O'Connor ran round the stage tailed by the Wicked Owl, he kept asking the audience, 'Where's the Owl ? Where's the Owl ?' At the sixth time of asking, a six-year-old issued a bossy injunction from the stalls, 'Don't tell him – the man's obviously an idiot.'

Mr O'Conner himself can be an eccentric member of an audience. 'With an image like mine,' he told the *Sunday Mirror*, 'you have to be on your guard twenty-four hours a day. I was in a club the other night, watching a comedienne's act. Suddenly she started coming out with a lot of blue material. People sitting near me kept turning round to check on my reaction. Either way I couldn't win. If I had sat silently with a disapproving look on my face, she would have been upset. If I had laughed at her jokes, the people would have thought my image was a sham.

'So I got up and walked out.'

As a member of an audience, Sir Ralph Richardson spoke disconcertingly as he found. Walking out of O'Toole's Macbeth half-way through, he announced loudly : 'It's not at all what you expect. It's like having a duff operation at the Middlesex.'

When Lenny Bruce appeared at The Establishment in 1963, the Irish actress Siobhan McKenna walked out angrily in the middle of his act and, spotting Peter Cook, the club's proprietor, in the foyer, she boxed him on the nose. The old satirist and keep-fit enthusiast had to be stretchered backstage for repairs.

Audience hooliganism has sometimes been caused by too convincing a performance. David Garrick is generally recognized as having been the first great naturalistic actor (when, as Macbeth, he told the actor playing the First Murderer, 'There's blood upon thy face,' he delivered the line so well that the startled First Murderer said: 'Is there, by God!'), but there are earlier accounts of actors being too good in a role. In Stockholm in the early sixteenth century, the actor playing Longinus in *The Mystery Of The Passion* had to pierce Christ on the cross. His performance was too realistic. The King of Sweden, who was present, was so incensed that he climbed on to the stage and cut off Longinus's head. The audience, who had been pleased with the actor's interpretation, rushed the stage and killed the king.

A nineteenth-century touring company was travelling through the United States with a production of *Othello*. In Chicago, Iago's behaviour so enraged a man in the stalls that he stood up with a cry of 'You rascal!' and shot him dead.

As the Big Bad Wolf began to menace Little Red Riding Hood and her grandma in a pantomime at Chesterfield, six-year-old Paul Farrow climbed on to the stage, punched Tim Fulstow, who was playing the wolf, and told him that he should be ashamed of himself.

On 10 August 1977, Warren Mitchell was giving a performance at the Criterion Theatre of *The Thoughts Of Chairman Alf*.
'What about *men's* lib, then? Sex ain't a thing the working

man's used to. You can't expect a man to entertain his wife after a hard day's work, can you? But if you're not satisfied with her, put her on the transfer list, like a bloody footballer. We *own* them, don't we, and we bloody train them.'

A woman in the audience jumped up squawking, 'Nobody owns *me*! *Nobody*, do you hear?'

'I can understand that,' said Alf. 'Nobody would *want* to bloody own you! Ha!'

Her bearded companion ran down the aisle, jumped on to the stage and took a swing at Alf, knocking his glasses off.

'I take it as a tribute to my acting that anyone should get so angry,' said Warren Mitchell. 'They were a pair of puddings.'

A complete absence of realism can be equally distracting, of course. When directing *Julius Caesar* at the Old Vic, Michael Benthall had occasion to rebuke the extras for their lack of authenticity. 'Just behave as you would normally in a crowded street,' he said. That night a member of the crowd walked off shouting 'Taxi!'

Bad Behaviour by Performers

Apart from the essentially self-adoring habit of giggling – or corpsing, as they're pleased to call it – performers can disrupt the mood of a piece in other and less half-witted ways, be it by drunkenness, retaliation, forgetfulness, vanity, horseplay or feuds, on-stage and off.

In 1718, James Quin, the leading actor of the day, took the title role in *Cato* at Lincoln's Inn Fields Theatre. A Welshman named Williams was to play the character of Decius, who entered with the line: 'Caesar sends health to Cato.' Instead of the classical pronounciation Quin expected, Williams spoke

'*Just behave as you would normally in a crowded street,*' he said . . .

unintelligibly in Welsh. Quin was astounded. 'Would they had sent me a better messenger !' he cried, and for the rest of the act made fun of Williams's accent, making jokes about leeks and so forth. The Welshman was enraged. In the interval he demanded an apology from Quin for ridiculing him in front of the audience. Quin refused, and kept up his banter for the rest of the evening. After the play, the Welshman lay in wait for Quin up an alley. As Quin approached, the Welshman jumped out with a cry of 'Ho!' and swung his sword. Quin drew his rapier and ran the Welshman through.

Joseph Jefferson once acted with the great Macready. 'Macready was acting Werner. I was cast for a minor part. In one scene a number of characters had to rush off, bearing lighted torches, in search of a delinquent. At rehearsal the tragedian particularly requested that we should all be sure and make our exit at night at just the same time and place, so that we might not disturb the arrangement of the scene. All went well until we made our hurried exit, when, to my horror, I found Macready standing exactly in line with my place of exit at rehearsal. I presume that when he gave his directions in the morning he did not observe me. The cue was given, and there was no time for argument. I rushed past him, torch in hand. I heard his well-known growl ; but as I flew by an unmistakable aroma of burnt hair filled the atmosphere, and I knew that I had set fire to his wig.

'The enraged Macready tore the wig from his head and stood gazing at it for a moment in helpless wonder. Suddenly he made a rush in my direction. The audience, seeing he was on the warpath, and that I was his game, cheered at the promise of a chase. I dodged him up and down the stage, over rocks and gauze waters. He never would have caught me but that in my excitement I ran headfirst into the stomach of a fat stage carpenter. Here I was seized, but the enraged Macready was so out of wind that he could only gasp and shake his wig at me.'

When touring in 1940 in J.B.Priestley's *Cornelius*, Dirk

Bogarde was so impressed by the modestly good notices he received that on the second night he tried to take over the play – rolling his eyes, posing in doorways and pulling faces. Unable to take this behaviour any longer, Max Adrian, playing the timid clerk, brought a heavy ledger down on Bogarde's head with a cry of '*Never* do that again, I say!' Bogarde, squint-eyed and spaghetti-legged, cannoned into a wall and slid unconscious to the floor. The audience applauded as loudly as the cast.

Early in his career, Noël Coward was engaged by Mr Cecil Barth to tour in *Charlie's Aunt* with Esme Wynn (Stoj) and Arnold Raynor. Mr Barth refused to let Coward share rooms with Raynor, because, he said, it would give the company a bad name. He was paired off with Stoj, while Raynor shared with Norah Howard. In Chester, Coward and Stoj had a row because he used her make-up. In Manchester they had another row because she'd forgotten to book digs, and in Wolverhampton Stoj finally lost her temper and knocked Coward down just before his entrance in Act III. He had no time to fight back and tottered on-stage with his collar torn and his white tie under his left ear. In the dressing-room afterwards he confronted Stoj: 'Now then, Stoj, we'll have this out,' he said, so she knocked him down again. Coward lost control and threw his make-up box at her. So she hit him again so hard that he banged his head against the wall and fell to the floor. Arnold Raynor rushed in at this point and hit Stoj on the head with a hairbrush. Then they all became friends.

In a BBC memorial programme devoted to Coward's life and work, Michael MacLiammoir popped up with a delightful tribute. Speaking of Coward's Slightly in *Peter Pan*, he said, 'He was very bad, even then.' (When MacLiammoir and Hylton Edwardes ran the Abbey Theatre, Dublin, they were known as Sodom and Begorrah.)

Performing the difficult Rose Adagio in *The Sleeping Beauty*, Alicia Jacks, New Zealand's leading ballerina, levelled, *en pirouette*, four supporting princes with one swing of her arm. Mr Brian Ashton, one of the princes, told a press conference that Miss Jacks had floored him on purpose and that lifting her was like picking up a plastic dustbin with no handles. Miss Jacks retaliated by saying that Mr Ashton padded his tights with sanitary towels.

In 1937, Eddie Cantor and George Jessell were topping the bill at the Palace Theatre, New York, and at the end of the show they did a routine together. One night Cantor made an unscripted joke that got a big laugh. Then Jessell topped him with an ad-lib that got an even bigger laugh. Cantor couldn't think of anything to say, so he took his shoe off and hit Jessell over the head with it. This got the biggest laugh so far. Jessell was upset. He walked down to the footlights and said, 'Ladies and Gentlemen. This so-called grown-up man, whom I have the misfortune to be working with, is so lacking in decorum, breeding and intelligence, that when he was unable to think of a clever retort he had to descend to the lowest form of humour by taking off his shoe and striking me on the head. Only an insensitive oaf would sink so low.'

Cantor hit him over the head again.

Gladys Cooper was only required for the last thirty minutes of *Milestones*, by Arnold Bennett and Edward Knoblock. In those days producers liked to get their money's worth, so the Vedrenne-Eadie Management hired her out to other theatres for first-act roles and special matinées. One month they lent her to Drury Lane, where she just had time to die affectingly as 'Beauty' in *Everywoman* before hurrying across London to do her bit in *Milestones*. Exhausted by this punishing schedule, she 'died' one night as Beauty and then fell sound asleep on stage. When an actor exited, banging the door behind him, she woke up with a start and said, 'What the hell was that?'

In 1962, Sybil Thorndike and Lewis Casson appeared in *Uncle Vanya* at Chichester. Casson was Waffles, and Dame Sybil

. . . levelled, en pirouette, four supporting princes . . .

played the Nurse. There being no curtain at Chichester, actors, at the end of a scene, simply got up and left the stage. As the scene ended in which Waffles played his guitar, Dame Sybil got up to leave, but Casson remained slumbering in his chair. 'Waffles, Waffles,' she called to him gently, but there was no movement. 'Waffles, Waffles,' she called again, louder this time. Still Sir Lewis remained snoozing. Eventually she called sharply, 'Lewis! Wake up you silly old fool!' He jumped to his feet and they exited.

As a young actor Paul Scofield played Malcolm in *Macbeth* at Stratford. One night he was chatting in Donald Sinden's dressing-room and missed his cue for the scene in which Macduff says, 'Your noble father's murdered,' and Malcolm replies, 'Oh, by whom?' They heard shouts and the stage manager suddenly appeared in Sinden's dressing-room. Scofield was up the stairs like a rocket and arrived on-stage just in time to be told by Macduff that his noble father was murdered. 'Oh . . .' said Scofield, and then he realized that he had a cigarette in his mouth. He removed it, threw it to the floor, stubbed it out and continued, ' . . . by whom?' Later it was pointed out to him that he had also forgotten to put his wig on.

On the first night of a Broadway play, George Nash was by no means sure of his lines. On tour, a feud had grown up between him and the prompter, so the prompter, eager to show that Nash didn't know the part, kept prompting him unnecessarily. On the sixth occasion, Nash walked to the wings, pulled the prompter to his feet and said, 'Since you know the part so well, you have a go.'

In Act II, when Nash began to flounder, the prompter

refused to help him at all. He sat in the wings, grinning crazily and doing monkey impressions. 'Give me a word,' hissed Nash desperately. The word supplied by the prompter was unrepeatable on stage. Nash went to the wings and kicked the prompter on the leg. The prompter threw the book down and pursued Nash to the middle of the stage. 'OK buster!' he screamed, 'that's a charge for you in the morning!'

When *The Reluctant Débutante* opened in Brighton with Wilfred Hyde-White and Celia Johnson, she had her lines off perfectly, but not so Hyde-White.

'What's the matter, darling?' said Miss Johnson, as per script, but there was no answer. The seconds ticked by. Hyde-White at last appealed piercingly to the corner.

'Come on, boy! Wake up! Give me a line, give me a line.'

'Poached eggs on toast,' said the prompter.

'Poached eggs on toast,' said Hyde-White with a sigh of relief.

Orson Welles was once appearing in an open-stage production of *Julius Caesar*, performed in tandem with *Antony And Cleopatra*. During a matinée of *Julius Ceasar*, the stage door opened and an actress called Madie Christians walked on to the stage. She wasn't appearing in *Julius Caesar*, and, forgetting there was a matinée, had returned to retrieve something she'd left on-stage during the morning's rehearsal of *Antony And Cleopatra*. She was wearing a leopard-skin coat and was carrying a Co-Op shopping-bag full of groceries. Realizing that she had walked in on a performance, she went down on one knee and placed a hand across her forehead in what she hoped was a suitably overwrought Shakespearean gesture.

Since there was no curtain, changes between scenes were effected by lights alone, and when these dimmed for the end of the stabbing scene, Madie tried to make her way back to the stage door. Unfortunately, she got hopelessly entangled with the senators manoeuvring into their next positions, so that when the lights came up she was still there with her Co-Op shopping-bag. She never got off. Throughout the entire performance the audience kept spotting her, crouching Shakespeareanly in her leopard-skin coat in different parts of the stage.

Beatrice Lillie once appeared on Broadway in, unusually for her, a straight play with a show-stopping set. Playing a titled lady of some seriousness, she made her entrance at the top of an immensely pompous staircase. The first-night audience dutifully applauded the set, and then they applauded Miss Lillie, eager to see how she would carry off a straight part. Instead of descending graciously to the stage, where others in the cast were waiting solemnly for the reading of a will, she paused half-way down the stairs, drew aside some heavy velvet curtains, peered out and said, 'Pissing down as usual.'

Appearing in a drawing-room comedy shortly after the war, Ralph Richardson suddenly alarmed everyone by saying, 'Is there a doctor in the house?'

A man in the audience stood up.

'How do you find the play, doctor?' asked Richardson, 'Feeble, don't you think?'

Edmund Kean was a tremendous drinker and usually had to be doused under a pump before a performance. If he was too drunk to go on himself, he'd sit in a box and heckle his understudy. Once, during a summer engagement at a provincial theatre, there was no understudy, so the manager announced that *Hamlet* would be played without the Prince. Sir Walter Scott was present and reported that it was afterwards agreed by the bulk of the audience to have been a great improvement.

On another occasion Kean stumbled through the first act of a play, but became pie-eyed in the interval. The usual dousing had no effect, so the manager apologized to the audience.

'Unfortunately Mr Kean will be unable to continue his performance tonight due to malaria.'

'I'll have a bottle of that myself, thank you,' called a voice from the gallery.

*She was wearing a leopard-skin coat and was carrying
a Co-Op shopping-bag . . .*

Robert Newton, a distinguished drunk, was appearing in a play in Manchester as old Queen Mary lay on her deathbed. After the matinée the stage manager told the cast that she was not expected to live through the day, in which case, he said, the evening performance would be cancelled. Newton got drunk as a monkey and, on returning to the theatre, discovered that Queen Mary was still alive. He could hardly keep upright during Act I and the audience were becoming restless when the stage manager ran on-stage.

'Ladies and gentlemen,' he cried. 'I have some very sad news. The Queen is dead.'

'Thank God!' cried Newton, keeling over with relief.

Between shows it was Newton's habit to sit in his dressing-room with a bottle of gin, stark naked except for his half-hose and suspenders. Touring in a play with Anna Neagle, he received a note from her inviting him to tea in her dressing-room, where she was receiving three local ladies who had just seen the matinée. Newton went as he was, naked but for his socks, and behaved impeccably: making polite conversation and handing round cucumber sandwiches. When it was time for the ladies to leave he insisted on escorting them down the passage, out of the stage door and into the street, where he hailed them a taxi and stood waving them *adieu*.

Newton was once touring in *Richard II* with another great actor, and serious drinker, Wilfrid Lawson. One lunchtime they staggered out of a pub as pissed as puddings and passed a fishmongers. Newton stared for a long time at the rows of cods' heads on the slab.

'By God, Wilfrid,' he said, 'we've got a matinée!'

Propping each other up, they somehow wove their way back to the theatre, where Lawson, with his codpiece back to front, staggered on as John of Gaunt.

'If you think I'm pissed,' he told the audience, 'wait till you see the Duke of York.'

Newton went as he was, naked but for his socks . . .

Richard Burton once met Wilfrid Lawson in a pub near the Arts Theatre, where Lawson was having one of his greatest triumphs in *John Gabriel Borkman*. After a few drinks he insisted that Burton come and see the matinée, and, since he didn't open the play, he sat with Burton in the stalls, offering a running commentary. 'Ah,' he said at last, 'this bit's good. This is where I come on.'

At the Old Vic in 1954, Richard Burton and John Neville alternated the parts of Othello and Iago. Celebrating too well one lunchtime, they returned to the theatre and both played Iago. The audience noticed nothing unusual, nor did Burton and Neville.

Gertrude Lawrence liked to drink, though the habit seldom affected her performance. An exception was the first night of *Conversation Piece* in Boston. She made her famous entrance and posed in the doorway while the audience applauded wildly.

'It's mother, isn't it?' cried the young actor playing opposite her. 'Mind your own fucking business,' she replied.

Accidents and Sudden Death

On 19 August 1896, *The Sketch*, concerned by the number of accidents caused by the Victorians' taste for elaborate sword fights, issued a solemn warning under the heading: *The Tragedy At The Novelty Theatre.*

'Both ancient and modern records can show many a stage mishap, though not of so serious a character as that which has just occurred. Upon the night of the first production of H.J.Byron's powerful drama *Michael Strogoff* on Tuesday last, Mr Charles Wintour, in the title role, bearing dispatches to the Russian Duke, was set upon by Ivan Ogareff, the villain of the piece, played by Mr James Fernandez, and a duel with daggers ensued, in the excitement of which Mr Wintour was stuck through. But, with admirable pluck, he fenced on till the curtain fell, expiring later in the wings.

'Only the other day, too, Mr Gordon Craig, playing Macduff, "laid on" with such an excess of zeal that the unfortunate Macbeth suffered somewhat severely about the head: but not so badly as the unlucky Macduff who lost both thumbs in his stage fight with the Macbeth of the great Macready.

'In an amateur performance of *Romeo And Juliet*, at the Cathedral Schools, Manchester, on 31 March 1981, Tybalt, making a lunge at Romeo, unhappily passed his sword clean through Lady Capulet with fatal results.

'Many years ago, an Italian artist named Dombardi, who was playing in *Antigone*, had to turn his sword from his father's breast to his own, and, in the excitement, plunged it into his own breast and dropped on the spot.

'Once in a Chinese theatre two actors fought a stage duel in earnest for love of the same woman, one being killed before the audience; but cases such as this of deliberate murder are rare. Only a few years ago, Mr Barton McGuckin, singing below his form in *Rienzi* at Liverpool, had a nice escape when one of the crowd, approaching him with an upraised dagger, lost his footing as he took the stage, and stabbed himself to death at the feet of the fortunate McGuckin.'

The Victorians considered flying sparks an important feature of a sword fight. Irving used to attach flints to the end of his blade to achieve this effect. When the advent of electricity coincided with a new production of *Romeo And Juliet* at Drury Lane, he had the weapon wired up to ensure that they would throw off sparks. When Romeo and Tybalt drew their swords, they were connected instantly with the national grid and leapt about like prawns on a hot-plate. The audience cheered, thinking they had never seen such a lively fight, but at future performances the swords were insulated with rubber handles.

Giovanni Mario, who invented elastic-sided boots and was once stabbed by a pimp called Prudent, was also the most celebrated tenor of the mid-nineteenth century. After an unsuccessful tour of North America, in the course of which he'd been buried, in mid-aria, under a snow-drift when the roof of a theatre collapsed in a storm, he decided to celebrate his return with the most spectacular production of *Les Huguenots* ever mounted. To improve a key scene he engaged some guardsmen to play troopers. When given the order to fire, they took aim and shot him dead.

In 1888, the most brilliant audience of the season crammed every corner of La Scala, Milan – agog to see Madame Patti and Madame Salchi sing together for the first time. At five o'clock the crowd outside the theatre was immense. When the doors opened at seven, the rush for seats was desperate. A little old lady, swept along in the upward charge, had a heart attack from the excitement and was dead before reaching the first landing. The spiralling upward momentum of the crowd carried her round corners, down corridors and up three further flights to the gallery, where she was wedged tightly between two enthusiasts. The next morning, friends were summoned to collect her.

In 1953, an audience in Lille applauded wildly for 32-stone opera singer M. René Verdière, who, as Samson in *Samson*

And Delilah, had just brought the temple down with no trouble at all. He walked on-stage to take a bow, and was felled by a posy thrown for Delilah from the gallery.

Bernard Shaw's *The Philanderer* opened at the Mermaid Theatre with a specially installed parquet stage, so highly polished that actress Jane Arden, on her entrance, skated straight into a lady in the stalls. Miss Arden was badly shaken and when her understudy took over she skated straight into the same lady, who left the theatre, taking herself to be the butt of some joke. Grit was applied to the stage during the interval.

At the Palace Theatre, Manchester, in 1959, Bruce Forsyth called a couple up from the audience to take part in the show. When he heard that they'd been married for fifty-one years, he gave Katie Lunn, 76, a packet of hankies and persuaded her husband, Sam, 79, to sing 'My Old Dutch'. As he sang 'We've been together now for forty years', Mrs Lunn collapsed. Bruce carried her off-stage, but she was already dead. Bruce had been Mrs Lunn's favourite comedian and her nine grand-children had bought her tickets for the show as a Christmas treat. Bruce was too upset to comment.

The first night of *Chaganog*, an evening of mime with Julian Chagrin and George Ogilvie, was saved from disaster by the show's finale – a daring leap by Chagrin from a twelve-foot rostrum into Ogilvie's arms at the end of a sword fight. Ogilvie, forgetting about the carefully rehearsed climax, mimed off and Chagrin swallow-dived on to the point of his head. The audience, who until this moment had been unimpressed by the chalk-faced mimes, roared their approval and stamped their feet. Chagrin was taken to hospital.

Actor Claude Jones fell three feet from the scenery on to the stage of London's New Theatre during a performance of *Oliver* and died before reaching hospital. Mr Jones, 60, was playing Dr Grimwig and four similar parts. He'd been in the show

. . . and was felled by a posy thrown for Delilah from the gallery.

since it opened thirteen weeks before – the longest run of his acting career. Mrs Jones, a dresser in another show, was given a matinée off to attend his funeral, but was docked a day's wages.

Sir John Gielgud played Hamlet for the last time at the Cairo Opera House in 1950. It was an emotional occasion for the great actor, and as he took the stage he thought: 'Well, this is the last time I shall play this glorious part. It must be an unforgettable experience.' At that moment, Horatio had an epileptic fit and fell into his arms. Sir John bundled him into the wings and called for a replacement. At last an understudy was discovered and, though dressed and made up for another part, and not knowing a line of Horatio's, was tipped hurriedly on to the stage. Sir John played both parts, more or less, for as long as possible, but when Horatio said, 'Look my Lord, it comes !' – referring to the Ghost – Sir John became exasperated and kicked him on the shin. 'You bloody fool,' he snapped, 'you're pointing in the wrong direction.'

The audience, taking this to be a knock-about version of the famous play, laughed politely through the rest of Gielgud's last Hamlet.

Singer Donald Peers was signing off with his theme song, 'By A Babbling Brook', when a torrent of water swept him off-stage. The cascade had come too soon. It was meant for the next act at the Queen's Theatre, Blackpool: a dramatic £100,000 waterfall scene with showgirls.

During a performance of *Golden Boy* at the London Palladium, dance captain Jacqui Daryl accidentally king-punched Mr Showbusiness, Sammy Davis Jr, causing the one-eyed star to go temporarily blind. Bravely continuing the routine, Mr Showbusiness skittled three dancers and knocked over a table before going head first into the stalls.

Reginald Poppy, playing a comic policeman in a pantomime at

'You bloody fool,' he snapped, 'you're pointing in the wrong direction.'

Leeds, hit leading comedian Whimsical Walker so hard over the head with his rubber truncheon that Whimsical Walker's teeth flew into the orchestra pit, hitting a violinist in the eye.

During a tour of Denmark in 1969, Mick Jagger, dressed in a cocktail frock, said, 'This one's for Brian' and, touching two microphones at once, received an electric shock that hurled him backwards into the rest of the group. He fell on top of Bill Wyman, who was knocked unconscious.

Engine Room Artificer, Bill Dodds, returning from Mrs Thatcher's Falklands adventure, got two weeks' leave from the Navy to get married. As his bride, Gwen, was working as an assistant to a husband-and-wife team of French acrobats, Bill decided to join the show as a stage-hand at the Royal Court Theatre, Warrington, where the act was appearing. A wire broke and one of the acrobats fell on top of Gwen. She was merely bruised, but Bill, running to her assistance, arrived on-stage in time to be knocked as flat as a pancake by the other acrobat. From the hospital bed where he spent the rest of his honeymoon, Falklands hero Bill gave the thumbs-up sign and said, 'That was hairier than Bomb Alley.'

As a show-stopping climax to his act, escape artist Paul Danvers was strapped into a straightjacket and swung upside down from a rope eighteen feet above the stage. The act should have ended with Paul making a miraculous escape while his assistant counted to a hundred. Instead, Paul swung backwards and forwards like a pendulum, colliding several times with the scenery and knocking himself out cold.

While appearing in his own play, *Romanoff And Juliet*, Peter Ustinov was invited to play tennis by Mr Romanov, Minister-Counsellor at the Soviet Embassy in London. Mr Romanov wanted revenge, he said, for having his name taken in vain. Ustinov was partnered by a Tory MP, while Romanov played with Comrade Korbutt, of whom little else is known.

It was raining heavily and the Tory MP said, 'We can't go on in this,' but Ustinov, not wishing to be seen as a running-dog and an effete representative of a decadent system, insisted they play. Ustinov served under-arm, but badly, yet was not the worst player on the court. The Tory MP had never played before. The USSR won and, in the course of the game, Ustinov hurt his back. He left the cast of his play and spent eight weeks strapped to a board. Told that he'd have to wear a corset for life, he tried it on for one day and then went to Paris, where a Rumanian lady walked up and down his spine. He grew over an inch and had to have all his trousers lengthened.

I once had an off-stage accident with the great raconteur myself, as it happens, though no West End productions, I think, were affected by it. On a honeymoon in France in '58, I bought a pornographic paperback, as one did in those days, and settled down to read it by the pool at *La Réserve*, Beaulieu, having first, for discretion's sake, wrapped it in a yellow Victor Gollancz cover advertising an anti-A-Bomb compilation, to which many distinguished people – Bertrand Russell, A.J.Ayer, Hugh Gaitskell and Philip Toynbee etc – had contributed. Ustinov, who was staying at the same hotel, walked past with Billy Rose, the New York showman, and, attracted by the Gollancz cover, stopped and said, 'How interesting. May I have a look ?' I could hardly refuse, so I handed him the book. He read one stupefyingly filthy paragraph, checked the names on the cover, read another paragraph, re-checked the names, and then handed the book back without a word. It must have been one of the few occasions on which the great conversationalist was stumped for a *mot* in any language.

In 1963 Nicol Williamson and Sarah Miles were appearing in a two-hander at the Royal Court Theatre. Walking to dinner after the show one night, Williamson decided to sing in Hans Place. An angry man stuck his head out of an upstairs window and told him to put a sock in it.

33

'Come down and say that to my face !' shouted Williamson, who likes to settle matters on the cobbles.

The window closed with a bang and thirty seconds later the smallest man Miss Miles claims to have seen outside of a circus tent ran into the street. Williamson went into a boxer's crouch and the little man punched him up the nose. Miss Miles managed to box the little man away and then carried Williamson home. He was off for three nights.

Unsuccessful Scenery, Exploding Props and Crazed Revolves

Playing Marguerite Gautier in *La Dame Aux Camelias* for the first time, Sarah Bernhardt had just arranged her guests at the dinner-table when the scenery collapsed on top of them. Their heads perforated the thin canvas and were held fast as the scene proceeded, sticking up like coconuts in an Aunt Sally. Later, at one of the play's more touching moments, Bernhardt was about to hand her lover a camelia when she noticed that the stage management had forgotten to provide one. She retired crossly to the wings to make good this oversight and then, with no time to check the prop, spoke her lines: 'Take this flower, Armand. It is a pale, cold, senseless thing, but purity itself,' and she handed him half a carrot that a confused ASM had been eating in the wings. At a later date, Bernhardt had one of her greatest triumphs in the role.

Actor Guy Middleton and actress Tottie Truman-Taylor were hit by five hundredweight of scenery just before the curtain went up on the first house of *Gentlemen Prefer Blondes* at the Princess Theatre, London. Tottie was taken to hospital, but

Guy Middleton, who had received a stupefying blow to the head and was suffering from double vision, refused first aid. 'I haven't missed a show in thirty-five years and I'm not going to miss this one,' he said, and, having lost all sense of spatial relations, walked head first into the orchestra pit, spearing a kettle-drum. A doctor said that Mr Middleton, who wore a David Niven moustache and, as a consequence, played silly-ass roles, had been saved from serious injury by his Homburg hat.

Arthur Marshall once attended the first night of an elaborate musical, based on a famous novel. 'There were ominous back-stage bumpings and bangings and lighting imperfections and unexplained pauses and loud whisperings. At one point, after the audience had been sitting quietly in darkness for some time, bright lights suddenly came on to reveal an empty stage on to which there shyly entered from the right a piece of scenery. I should like to say it glided on, but to tell the truth, judder on was what it did, propelled on some sort of trolley. It was quite a large piece of scenery and it showed us the side of a town house, with front door and windows and steps and a small yew tree. It came to rest, in full view, and a respectful silence fell. We gazed politely at it, and it gazed right back at us. The silence backstage was now complete, and one felt that they must have all gone out for a cup of tea, or home perhaps. After at least two minutes the scenery juddered to life and made its way back to the wings, never to be seen again. The audience clapped politely.'

Hair was presented in Holland by an English producer who, at the time, was kept going, more or less, by electro-convulsive shock therapy powered by a pocket dynamo hidden under his waistcoat. Three days before the opening it was brought to his attention that he had forgotten to book a theatre, though he had remembered to invite the Dutch Royal Family to the first night. A circus tent was hired, and bench seats hastily erected. The latter, unfortunately, were balanced faultily, causing a see-saw effect. When the Dutch Royal Family arrived, the audience stood up. The Dutch Royal Family waved graciously and sat down. Then the audience sat down and the Dutch Royal Family were shot into the air like tumblers on a variety bill. At this point the band decided to play the National Anthem. The audience stood up, the bench seats pivoted the other way, and the Dutch Royal Family sprawled untidily in the saw-dust. This might have gone on all night had not Dutch creditors with pocket calculators arrived at that moment to take the set, costumes and lighting back. The show was cancelled.

In 1960 I produced a revue, written and directed by John Bird, called *Here Is The News*, an uncompromising evening, billed, dauntingly, as 'An Eleventh Hour Comment'. It opened in Coventry in Wakes Week, a time, apparently, when audiences in the area expect Cannon and Ball and girls in tights. Bird's was a dark entertainment, made darker by the fact that there was no lighting at all. Bird thought that the designer, Sean Kenny, was doing it; Kenny thought Bird was; and I, being new to the dodge, didn't know there was such a thing as lighting. The first sketch had to do with the appalling consequences of a nuclear explosion (as did all the others, come to that) and ended with the entire cast, including Cleo Laine, Shiela Hancock, Lance Perceval and Richard Goolden, 86, being 'blown up' into the roof on wires. Robin Ray, the dapper musicologist, got stuck and spent the rest of the evening up there, with just his pumps showing. Perhaps he was fortunate. The rest of the cast, since the show was performed in a permanent black-out, spent the next two hours walking into the scenery and falling off the stage. By the interval the theatre was empty except for the critic of the *Birmingham Post* who reported in the morning that the show was an unqualified triumph.

Wires are always a hazard, leaving *ingénues* standing while whipping their dresses into the roof, removing toupeés from leading men and hooking the wrong people in the wings – even the stage-staff – and casting them promiscuously across the stage. Ernest Thesiger, a fine old actor, being unable, through age, to make it to his dressing-room between one scene and the next, used to sit in the wings doing embroidery, at which he was expert. In a play involving flying, he was sewing quietly in the wings in an old woolly when a harness, meant for another and younger mime, fished him out of his chair and swung him, clutching his embroidery, into the action.

Donald Sinden tells of a production of *The Tempest* at Stratford in which nothing went right. When Prospero, addressing Ariel, said: 'Then to the elements be free,' Ariel was meant to walk a few paces, turn back to Prospero, with tears in his eyes, turn away again and fly out of sight. Instead of disappearing silently, he hit the scenery and came swinging back at the un-suspecting Prospero, already launched on his next speech, knocking him flat from behind.

Sometimes, according to Arthur Marshall, flying mishaps have been purposely brought about. When Gladys Cooper was playing Peter Pan, she had contrived to make herself unpopu-lar backstage. Those responsible for flying her decided on revenge. One evening in the Darlings' nursery, as Peter was demonstrating to Wendy his airborne skills, the stage staff, instead of landing Miss Cooper neatly on the chimney-piece, swung her backwards and forwards across the stage, bouncing her off the walls like a wrecking-ball on a building site. (Miss Cooper must have been basically sound, because she once bit Dirk Bogarde's head.)

When the Alberts – masters of complicated props and exploding devices – mounted *The Three Musketeers* at the Arts Theatre Club in 1966, they built an enormous mousetrap in which, at an exciting moment in the play, the wicked Cardinal Richelieu would be caught. They also engaged a Russian for the part of D'Artagnan. He couldn't speak English, but they wanted him to do authentic Russian dances in exploding boots. The joke would be that the more energetically he danced the more his boots would explode, and *vice versa*. At a lunch-break in rehearsals, the dynamite used in this and other tricks was left by an open window in a dressing-room. The sun ignited it and the doors were blown off the cubicles in the Gents next door. Stratford Johns, crouching over a crossword, emerged as white as cod-roe, vowing never to eat at the Arts again. Mr Birtwhistle, formerly the proprietor of a snooker-room in the north, but now enjoying his first day as the proud new owner of the Arts, was showing off to some business cronies in the restaurant. Hurrying boastfully to investigate – 'Leave this to me !' – he was caught in the mousetrap, left lying in an aisle, and was held fast until the Alberts came back from their lunch two hours later.

In the course of a pantomime at the Yvonne Arnaud Theatre, Guildford,* the Wicked Fairy was concocting an evil spell over a bubbling cauldron. With a final triumphant 'Abracadabra !' she brought the spell to its peak, but instead of turning the Good Fairy into a jelly, a faulty electronic flash under the cauldron blew the Wicked Fairy's knickers off. Property Mistress, Mrs Dolly Dawkins, admitted she was having a bad trot. The previous year an exploding oven had blown Mother Hubbard twenty feet across the stage.

In a pantomime at the Tivoli Theatre, Melbourne, it was the Good Fairy who caught fire. Actress Gabriel Hartley was

* Named after the fine comedienne who always claimed she couldn't speak English but on at least one occasion proved she was familiar with the folk-lore of her adopted country. Seeing Evelyn Laye lying on the ground in a field, she said: 'Doesn't that mean it's going to rain ?'

meant to materialize out of a puff of smoke, but she claimed in court that what happened ruined her career. She told the jury that her fairy's costume caught fire in a blast from a faulty stage effect and that burns disfigured her arms, back and legs. She said she had complained several times to the management about the prop being over-loaded and added that an eighteen-year-old stage-hand who looked after the flash-pot often taunted her with remarks like: 'It'll be a beaut tonight, darling.'

Two weeks before the accident she had become engaged, but her fiancé had broken it off, she told the court, and had now returned to England. Gabriel said she was quitting the stage to become an undertaker.

The most spectacular accident caused by a mad revolve occurred on the first night at Sir Oswald Stoll's newly opened Coliseum in 1904. The Derby was to be re-enacted on stage, complete with crowds, pickpockets, toffs, bookmakers, mounted police and six horses ridden by professional jockeys on a revolving platform. Due to a fault in its braking mechanism, the revolve, which was supposed to turn at a sensible fifteen miles per hour, gradually worked up speed until it was a blur to the eye. Jockeys, horses, bits of scenery, pickpockets, toffs and their ladies hurtled across the footlights, causing the audience to duck and weave. Miraculously there was only one fatality. Leading jockey Fred Dent, in Lord Derby's colours, went like a rocket into the side of a box and died before reaching Charing Cross Hospital.

The Derby was run again the next night with a safety-net strung across the footlights.

In 1963, Oscar Brown Jr – creator of *Kicks And Co*, and thought, at the time, to be the smartest thing on either side of the Atlantic – was brought over to England at some expense to star with Annie Ross in a jazz revue called *Wham Bam Thank You Mam*. The first night was quite an occasion, and buffs in the audience waited eagerly for their first glimpse of the fabled

Jockeys, horses, bits of scenery, pickpockets, toffs and their ladies hurtled across the footlights . . .

Mr Brown. At the end of the opening number, which included everyone except the star, the cast was revolved off and, to thunderous cheers and cries of 'Wow!' and 'Hey! Hey! Hey!' from the buffs, Oscar was revolved on singing 'Mr Kicks'. 'Permit me to introduce myself, my name is Mr Kicks,' he sang, the audience screamed, and Oscar was unaccountably revolved off, still singing but looking surprised. At the back of the revolve was Fred Emney, who, having neither the time nor the wind to make it to his dressing-room, was changing for his next number. On he came, a fat man in a top hat, struggling out of his trousers and startled to find himself in the spotlight. He was revolved off, and back came Oscar, now into the second verse of 'Mr Kicks', but no sooner was he on, than he was off again, to be replaced once more by the trouserless Mr Emney. The two of them were revolved on and off thirty-two times, and might still be revolving today had not the company manager, Griffith James, run on-stage with an axe and smashed the revolve to bits.

Intending to mark his appointment as conductor of the Atlanta Symphony Orchestra with an unforgettable performance, Mr Robert Shaw installed sixteen electronically fired mini-canons throughout the auditorium. Half-way through the 1812 Overture he pressed the button marked 'Fire Cannon One', whereupon all sixteen fired together, stunning the fifteen thousand-strong audience and filling the great dome with smoke.

Hardly had the music-lovers staggered to their feet when the 'Smell-All-Tell-All Customer Safety System' drenched them with anti-burn foam. They escaped into the foyer, only to be brutally driven back into the burning auditorium by the Atlanta Emergency Fire-Fighting Crew, who charged into the theatre with cries of 'Geronimo!'

'I have to admit to a number of incidents,' said Fire Captain Bronski. 'The fighters were wearing a new model smoke-mask and couldn't see what they were doing.'

Sir Raph Richardson, who liked nothing better than a loud bang, once reduced the Oliviers' drawing-room to rubble with a firework he'd brought from London. As a young actor he joined F.R.Growcott's company and one of his first jobs was to simulate a Zeppelin raid in a wartime comedy which Growcott himself had written. He was given a stick of dynamite and told to hide himself in a small space underneath the stage. The signal for the explosion was to be Growcott tapping on the stage with a stick. But Growcott, who was very short, wore lifts, and Richardson, crouched under the stage, was confused by Growcott's curious tapping gait as he made his first entrance and mistook it for his cue. Before Growcott could deliver his opening line, Richardson went into action and blew him twenty feet into the air.

Failed Tricks and Unsuccessful Novelty Acts

Harry Houdini, the great escapologist, announced from the stage that he could withstand any blow to the abdomen, however vicious.

'I am strong as an ox!'

A fan climbed on to the stage and boxed him in the stomach. The great illusionist collapsed on the spot and died hours later of peritonitis . The audience demanded their money back.

Miss Rita Thunderbird, the human cannon-ball, performs in a gold lamé bikini. At Battersea in 1977, a large and appreciative audience cheered as Miss Thunderbird climbed down the gun-barrel. There was a loud explosion. Miss Thunderbird remained lodged in the cannon while her knickers were blown across the Thames.

Roy Rogers was hit by flying saucers and shot his horse Trigger during the last performance at the King's Theatre, Edinburgh. Rogers, using a revolver loaded with pellets, was firing at saucers thrown into the air by the audience. Several saucers hit the singing cowboy and, while trying to dodge them, he shot Trigger – the horse with human knowledge – up the arse.

Engaged by Mohammed Fal, Master of Ceremonies at the Court of Jeddah, to perform at the birthday party of Prince Aziz, Mr George Turner, known professionally as Merlin the Magnificent, said:

'Knowing that Royalty would be present, I was determined to give everything I could. Then Mr Fal told me that I should perform the Guillotine Yourself At Home Illusion – one of the hardest in a conjuror's repertoire. I replied that perhaps it would be better if, as the high point of the show, we stoned a rabbit to death, whereupon I was deported.'

The hypnotist Romark announced in 1977 that he was going to give a public display of his psychic powers.

'I am going to drive blindfold through Ilford,' he said.

On 12 October he placed two coins, a slice of dough and a thick band across his eyes. Then he climbed into a yellow Renault and set off down Cranbrook Road. After twenty yards he drove into the back of a parked police car. A large, admiring crowd formed round Romark, who said: 'The car was parked in a place that logic told me it wouldn't be.'

Mr Lemmy Chipowe, a magician from Chingola, Zambia, assured a small crowd that if anyone gave him one Zambian pound they could bury him alive for two and a half hours. A Mr Fitula, also of Chingola, gave him the money and helped to bury him. Having waited for the time to elapse, the crowd dug him up. He was dead. His wife said, 'Something must have gone wrong.'

A packed theatre at the Grove Theatre, Belfast, watched tensely as pretty Violet O'Leary was bundled into a trick trunk by magician Horace MacGillicuddy and hoisted twenty feet above the stage. When Violet, 22, failed to make her escape, Horace called for help. Stage-hands ran on and lifted Violet out of the trunk. She was unconscious.

'I suffer from claustrophobia,' she explained later. 'As soon as I was locked inside the trunk I fainted.'

Violet, a sales clerk, had stepped into the show at the last minute when Horace's original partner fell ill.

The Least Successful Hypnotist

At the Gaumont, Southampton, in 1978, hypnotist, the Great Orlando, announced that he would put twenty volunteers from the audience into a trance. 'You are going into a deep sleep,' he told the first subject, local electrician Bob Holliday. Mr Holliday remained alert, but the Great Orlando did a duck impression and then admitted to being Mr George Rowson, wanted by the police of four counties for social security frauds.

Mr Holliday is thinking of taking up the business professionally.

The Least Successful Pickpocket

Having performed his pickpocketing act for the warders and their wives at Wormwood Scrubs Prison in December 1961, the Amazing Adam returned home without his watch, truss, glasses, braces and money-belt.

The Least Successful Impressionist

Invited to dinner at Kensington Palace, Michael Holroyd was warned that Princess Margaret liked to set the table on a roar with her skilful impressions. At her first attempt, the celebrated biographer screamed with laughter and banged the table. She had been speaking in her normal voice.

The Least Successful Elephant

While passing Olympia, where Bertram Mills' Circus was playing a Christmas season, the Countess of Dalkeith got stuck in a traffic jam. Irritated by exhaust fumes, an elephant standing directly in front of her vehicle relieved itself over the bonnet.

The Least Successful Elephant Trainer

At Las Vegas in 1982, Adolf Heinkel failed to call the theatre's vet when Dolores, one of his dancing elephants, became so blown with flatulence that she became almost twice her normal size.

'As is usual in such cases,' said Mr Heinkel, 'I inserted a large hose up Dolores's end and when it reached her stomach I applied a match. To my surprise, I was blown twenty feet backwards by a jet of flame, which set fire to the elephants' dressing-room. In next to no time it was a pile of ash.'

Dolores escaped with shock.

The Least Successful Sword Swallower

After a fish dinner at 'The Contented Sole', Margate, sword swallower The Great Fakir missed three performances of *Summer Follies 83*. He was in hospital having a fish-bone removed from his throat.

Briefed to heckle Bernard Manning at the Liverpool Empire, Wilfred Musprat, an ex-music-hall comedian currently on Manning's pay-roll, pitched up by mistake at Liverpool's Royal Court Theatre, where Topol was appearing in *Fiddler on the Roof*.

'If I were a rich man,' sang Topol. 'Dobeedobeedo-beedo . . . .'

'What are you going to do for a face when King Kong wants his backside back?' shouted Musprat from from a box.

God's Mysterious Ways

In the course of an entertainment performed in front of the Roman Emperor Diocletian (AD 245–313), Genesius, the finest actor of the day, took the lead in a mocking representation of the Christian baptism. In the course of the performance he was touched by the grace of God and, when presented to the Emperor, declared that he had been converted to Christ. He was beheaded on the spot.

Elizabeth Billington (1765–1818) was an English singer with a voice of remarkable sweetness. When travelling in Italy she was engaged to sing in Naples. As she made her entrance, Vesuvius erupted, causing the Neapolitans to suppose that God was expressing his displeasure at a Protestant performer. They stormed the stage and killed her.

When Oscar Panizza's irreligious satire, *Council D'Amour*, was presented at the tiny Criterion Theatre in 1970, the producers had got their arithmetic wrong. The cast – God, fairies, randy cardinals, wrestlers, nude Popes, Christ, tumblers, girls lobbing from nowhere and biting one another in the box – was so extensive that the play would have lost £4,000 a week playing to capacity. The larger the audiences, paradoxically, the more quickly the producers would have gone bankrupt. God intervened on their behalf. The Dowager Lady Birdwood – enthusiastically seconded by Lord Ampthill, heir to the grocery millions – brought a private prosecution under the 1376 Blasphemy Act, by which, if found guilty, the play's blameless choreographer, the great and wonderful Eleanor Fazan, would have been burnt at the stake as a witch. John Mortimer appeared, as so often, for the accused, the action failed humiliatingly and old Lady Birdwood was rebuked by the magistrate (George Robey's grandson, as it happened) for wasting the court's time. Meanwhile, the play, which was clearly in contempt of court, had been withdrawn, allowing the producers to escape with their fancy women to Morocco, where they opened a pub selling Watney's Red Barrel.

Shortly before the curtain was due to go up on a performance of *La Traviata*, specially mounted in honour of Pope John Paul II, leading soprano Andrea Guiot telephoned the theatre to say that she had influenza. No sooner had a replacement been found than baritone Julien Giovanetti rang to say that he too was ill. Thirty minutes later, Giovanetti's wife called the theatre to say that he had died of a heart attack. When contralto Helia T'Hezan reached the theatre and heard of Giovanetti's death she had hysterics and decided that she couldn't go on. Her understudy, Denise Montell, was rushed to theatre while the audience waited, but was caught in a traffic jam. The Theatre manager wanted to cancel the show, saying it was jinxed. Leading tenor Alexandre Mazota would have none of it. 'Jinxed? Pah! Jinxed!' he cried, and, striding on-stage, he fell through a trap-door, broke his leg and was carried from the theatre on a stretcher.

'I was selling flowers on the corner of Montpellier Road,' said Mrs Rose Huggins, 63, 'when a man came up to me and said:

"I am God – could you direct me to the Brompton Oratory?" When I gave him the directions he took off his hat, said "thank you", stepped into the road and was run down by a cyclist.'

Actor Leslie Drinkwater, playing the voice of God in a miracle play to be performed in the grounds of the Oratory, died before reaching St. Stephen's Hospital.

In order to compete for a Golden Harp, a religious trophy awarded as part of the Roman Catholic Holy Year, with reconciliation as its theme, thirty provincial choirs assembled and performed before the judge, the Reverend Father de Liss, in Lusaka Cathedral. After the final round, sung between the Kimbu and Dara village choirs, the Reverend de Liss announced that the Kimbu Choir's rendering of 'Good Shepherd Lead Thy Peaceful Flock' had been surpassed by no more than a whisker by the Dara choir's 'Love Thy Neighbour, Love Thy Lord'. The decision was unpopular. Inspector Empibo of Lusaka police said: 'By the time we reached the Cathedral both choirs were involved in a pitched battle. The choirboys, average age forty, were using chairs and pews to bring their opponents to their senses. The judge had his clothes torn off his back and as far as I'm concerned, the future of the event lies in the balance.'

In 1953, Eliot's *Murder In The Cathedral* was performed in the chapel at Winchester College. Playing Becket was Father Anthony Bliss SJ, a keen amateur actor. Suddenly there was a cry of 'Fire!' Looking around him, the distinguished priest discovered that it was he who was alight. In his passion he had swayed backwards into a lighted candle. He finished the play sitting in a font. Afterwards he said, 'This goes to show that God has an agreeable sense of humour.'

In twelve months of rehearsals for a one night show, members of the Galathea Dance Company were hit by two broken marriages, a plague of boils, a series of mystery accidents and the destruction of taped background noises on the show's £23,000 sound equipment.

'It's like a curse,' said former dancer Marie Clery, writer and producer of the musical play *Nazerene* at Selsey Bill, Sussex. 'The Holy Spirit's divorce is going through, and so is Mary Magdalene's.'

Rehearsals for the show in Selsey's Embassy Ballroom shouldn't have lasted as long as they did.,

'Players fell ill every other week,' said Marie. 'John the Baptist sat on a nail and Margaret Morgan, who plays the Holy Spirit, suffered a prolonged attack of boils.'

Mary Magdalene's husband Terence, 49, confirmed that their marriage was over. 'It is as though an evil stranger has come into our lives,' he said, speaking from the detached house in Selsey where he still lives with their two young children.

One of the few members of the cast of forty-three to escape unscathed was bank worker Bill Hammond, 38, who played Satan. Builder John Stanley, who played Christ, said, 'Something Satanic has crept in. When we used the Medmerry Junior School for rehearsals, an aquarium exploded, killing all the fish.'

Eccentric TV astronomer Patrick Moore – a favourite with audiences at local amateur shows – dismissed the idea of the Selsey jinx as a lot of nonsense.

'I know people think we're all potty in Selsey,' he said. 'I steer clear of trouble by sticking to Gilbert and Sullivan.'

Suddenly there was a cry of 'Fire!'

Audience Participation

The Living Theatre Company – low-life types without electricity, many of whom in their time have lived co-operatively with goats – are followers of Antonin Artaud, who invented the Theatre of Cruelty and spent nine years in asylums for the seriously nervous, receiving fifty electric shocks, which resulted in his losing all his teeth. Believing, with the master, that the audience should suffer with the actors, the Living Theatre Company, touring South Wales with an anti-nuclear weapons drama, decided to go all out for audience participation. On the first night in Swansea, they left the stage and staggered among the audience, simulating death by radiation. The audience became restless. Words were exchanged. Chairs were smashed. Fists flew. The Living Theatre Company retreated to the stage, but had taken such a beating that they were unable to complete their pacifist drama.

'As far as I'm concerned,' said director, Chris Keeble, 'Swansea is a cultural desert.'

In *Nights At The Comedy*, Dan Farson's courageous attempt to bring pub entertainment to the West End, the audience were offered, among other marvels – including Jimmy James, Ida Barr and the incomparable Mrs Shufflewick – a fiver if they could hit Arthur Howard, then a contender for the British middleweight title, on the nose. Having been assured that Arthur, whose fists, since he was a professional, were legally classified as offensive weapons, wouldn't hit back, two sailors from Plymouth climbed on to the stage, and one of them immediately caught Arthur a terrific crack, plumb on the button. Arthur, who was a bit punchy, forgot the no-retaliation guarantee and chased the sailors all over the stage, finally catching them in a corner and giving them a frightful dumping.

As possible accessories to a grievous bodily harm charge, the management – myself, as it happens – dispensed with Arthur's services and engaged those of Wladek 'Killer'

Kowalski, a stone-bald wrestler who bounced for the Nash brothers. He looked terrifying, but in fact had the disposition of a pussy-cat and had long outgrown his strength. A fiver was offered to anyone who could beat him in the best of three falls, whereupon a little old lady, who, unbeknown to the management, was a martial arts black belt, ran on to the stage and took him in a judo hold. Killer Kowalski picked her up and threw her back into the stalls. He too was dismissed, and went back to bouncing for the Nash brothers.

Policeman's wife Mrs Mary Skupski, 26, and mother-of-two Pat Alexander, 37, claimed they were tricked on to the stage at Blighty's Club in Bolton, Lancs, by comedian Pete Mack.

'When the compère asked for us by name we thought we'd won a prize,' said Mrs Alexander. 'Instead he cracked blue jokes and pulled our knickers down. Then he said we wouldn't be allowed to leave until we helped him undress.'

Mrs Alexander, of Bleasdale Road, Mossley Hill, Liverpool, added: 'Eventually Mrs Skupski pulled his shirt off and I helped with his trousers.'

But the ordeal for the embarrassed housewives of Liverpool's Palmerston Tennis Club wasn't over. They claimed that compère Mack then ordered them to dance the can-can.

Said Mrs Skupski: 'When I said I wouldn't, he tried to pluck my skirt up.'

Compère Mack said: 'My humour can be a bit earthy, but this is the first time I've had a complaint.'

Unintended Audience Participation

In 1974 a young woman attended a performance of the rock musical *Godspell* at Wyndham's Theatre. During the interval the cast invited members of the audience up on to the stage to meet them. The young woman left her seat, walked down the arcade outside and through the stage door. After climbing a flight of stairs she turned right and found herself on a brilliantly lit stage. She was in *Pygmalion* at the Albery Theatre next door.

The Marquis and Marchioness of Tavistock and an audience of smart theatre-lovers, attending an open-air charity performance of *A Midsummer Night's Dream* in the grounds of Woburn Abbey, were roused from their torpor when a man dressed as Adolf Hitler ran on-stage and cried, 'Was ist going on?'

Speaking from the dock Mr I.S.Hinchcliffe said: 'I had been wandering round for several hours looking for a fancy-dress ball promised by invitation. I thought I had found it at last.'

Mr Herbert Dell, presiding, said: 'We don't like this sort of thing in Woburn. The maximum fine is ten pounds. I fine you ten pounds.'

The stage door of the Oxford Playhouse opens on to an alleyway, on the opposite side of which is a pub. During a performance of *West Side Story* in 1972, Maria and the girls were trying on dresses and singing 'I Feel Pretty' when they were joined by a dancing First World War veteran, who, staggering out of the pub, had been drawn into the theatre by the sound of a musical knees-up. Nothing could get him off the stage, and later in the show he teamed up with the Sharks in the big rumble against the Jets, inflicting some damage in spite of his condition.

In the old days Nottingham had a music-hall and a theatre side by side. Topping the bill at the music-hall was an escapologist who, as a finale to his act, was chained and padlocked inside a trunk. The trunk was then carried on to the roof of the theatre, whence he would escape to reappear on stage within minutes. On his first night in Nottingham, the escapologist got out of

'Was ist going on?'

the trunk, ran down the fire-escape, dashed through the open stage door and ran on-stage in the middle of an Edgar Wallace thriller shouting, 'Here I am! Here I am!'

After a career rocked by law-suits, illnesses, controversy, broken marriages and suicide bids, Judy Garland fell over her dog and broke an arm just days before her big come-back at Hollywood's outdoor Greek Theatre in 1965. After a three-week postponement, the big night came round again, but Judy was upstaged by a skunk that wandered on-stage and refused to leave.

When I bought Jack Waller Ltd in 1958, I inherited Waller's old general manager, Bert Leywood, who had once been half of a novelty act with his wife Iris. I treated him impertinently and he, not being able to remember my name, used to call me 'the boy'. He never showed much interest in what I might be up to, but, hearing I was down in Brighton with a show called *Beyond The Fringe*, unaccountably decided to investigate. He caught the train to Brighton and, thinking I'd be at the theatre, but not realizing there was a matinée, wandered on-stage in the middle of an audacious anti-hanging sketch shouting, 'Where's the boy? Where's the boy?' Then he fell over a stage-weight and had a nose-bleed. I was mortified, but Dr Jonathan Miller, handily present, was able to administer first aid, before continuing the sketch.

Unsuccessful Charity Shows

The urban council at Stanley, near Wakefield, recently decided to raise £3,000 with a charity show at the Wakefield Theatre Club.

Among the guests were teachers, clergymen, Meals On Wheels staff and the Bishop of Wakefield, Dr Eric Treacy. After the Bishop's address they all sat down to enjoy the show. First on was cockney Mastermind Fred Housego, who immediately startled the audience by showing them his bottom.

The embarrassed council had to apologize, but a club spokesman said: 'I can't understand the fuss. It was more subtle than Fred's usual jokes.'

When Nicholas Parsons gave a charity show at Basingstoke in 1979, half the audience of pensioners walked out in protest.

Roland Edwards, a member of the charity committee, said: 'I'm no fuddy-duddy, but the show was the crudest I've ever seen.'

One 84-year-old grandmother said she was so disgusted she wanted to box Mr Parsons's ears.

'My act is as clean as a whistle,' said Mr Parsons. 'I've been in the business for fifty years.'

In the course of the evening, the charity chairman attempted to sell raffle tickets – the first prize being dinner with Mr Parsons at Basingstoke's best restaurant. There were no takers, but one old lady said, 'If I win, can I go by myself twice?'

In June 1974, singer Dorothy Squires had to cancel plans for a charity show at The Talk Of The Town because, she said, she had been snubbed not just by royalty but by the horse racing world too. She had hoped to sell 750 tickets at £25 each to help an appeal she had launched for the injured jockeys fund. But after nine weeks only three tickets had been sold.

'I am two thousand pounds out of pocket,' said Miss Squires. 'Now I intend to hire the Albert Hall. That can hold 6,500 people.'

When Terry Scott compèred a charity show at Quaglino's in 1972, he was driven off-stage by a barrage of bread-rolls thrown by the audience.

'I took a couple of Hooray Henrys by the lapels,' said Terry, 'but no one would admit to being the ring-leader. It's true I trod on a titled lady's head, but I didn't realize she was sitting on the floor.'

In the early seventies, Sir Richard Attenborough, as he then wasn't, arranged a charity performance in a church hall in aid of the Manchester Royal Exchange Theatre. After the show some thirty of our most dependable middle-order mimes – Frank Windsor, Stratford Johns, Geoffrey Keen, Rupert Davies, Barry Foster, Gerald Harper, Jon Pertwee, Pat Phoenix, Una Stubbs, etc – much pleased with their efforts and swapping anecdotes, left together by a side-door and walked into a septic tank.

Mr George Maguire, who had installed twenty temporary lavatories for the occasion, said: 'That's show business.'

A galaxy of household names – Bet Lynch, Joyce Blair, Edmund Hockridge, Kenny Lynch and Jimmy Tarbuck – offered to give their services free at a charity spectacular in aid of the 'Save A Toddler Fund'.

The organizers calculated that they would have no difficulty filling the 2,000-seat Liverpool Empire and raising £15,000. However, a NUPE official at the Liverpool hospital where the charity was based disapproved of the fact that Liverpool-born comic Jimmy Tarbuck, who had appeared alongside Mrs Thatcher at a Tory Party rally, was taking part in the show.

The official, Mr Peter Ballard, NUPE secretary for the Sefton division of Liverpool, recommended that no union member should buy tickets for the show. Posters were torn down, and only 387 seats were filled.

During his time as Commissioner of the Metropolitan Police, Sir Robert Mark attended a charity concert at the London Palladium in aid of the Police Widows' Fund. Lady Mark, who was wearing a red weasel fur and a hat with a pineapple on it, was mistaken for Hylda Baker and redirected to the *artistes'* entrance, and Sir Robert, who was wearing his uniform with a whistle in the top pocket, was taken to be the doorman. Until he was rescued by Lord Delfont and taken to a box, punters handed him their coats and offered him change to park their cars.

In 1950, Stewart Grainger and Diana Dors were engaged to open a charity tea-dance at the Grand Hotel, Broadstairs. Chatting to Alderman Norris before the do, and somewhat stuck for small-talk, Stewart Grainger thought it might amuse the Alderman to know that his real name was James Stewart and that Miss Dors had been born Diana Fluck. 'But don't get it wrong when you introduce us,' he said.

Moments later Alderman Norris stepped forward and announced: 'Ladies and Gentlemen. We are very privileged to have with us today Mr Stewart Grainger and Miss Diana Clunt.'

Unsuccessful Talent Contests

After his singing failed to win first prize at a local talent contest, Mr Edward Barefoot was assaulted by his wife Constance.

'I had great hopes for him,' said Mrs Barefoot. 'It was a 'Go-As-You-Please' contest, and I had made him promise to sing 'Happy–Go-Lucky Me' – one of our favourites. But when he reached the microphone he insisted on singing *Mon Amour* – in French. Needless to say, nobody present liked that sort of thing. So when he came back to his seat I hit him over the head with a hammer.'

Invited to compete in a festival devoted to discovering ethnic talent, the ochre-daubed warriors of Okapa, New Guinea, were so surprised at not being awarded first prize that they shot arrows into the audience of jet-set tourists. Without more ado, the attendants, who were riot police in disguise, charged the stone-age tribesmen. The Okapa warriors stood their ground. It was not until the tourists joined forces with the police that the performers were overwhelmed and chased back into the jungle.

Appearing in a senior citizens' away-day talent contest in Bognor, 76-year-old Bert Hodges stepped forward and recited:

> A robin redbreast on my sill
> Sang for a crust of bread.
> I slowly brought the window down
> And smashed his fucking head.

'I do not think this is the sort of material that should be used in front of a holiday audience,' said Mr Arthur Helmes, talent organizer and chairman of the judges.

'The verse is well known in theatrical circles,' protested Mr Hodges, who had once been on the halls.

Explaining why she had walked naked on to the stage at Scarborough in front of a holiday audience and recited, 'Get off the table, Mabel, the money's for the beer,' Miss Tina Forsyth, the amateur quick-change *artiste*, said:

'I had intended to do "Queens of England – 1066 to the present day", which I had been rehearsing for a year. But I discovered half an hour before the contest that my mother had sent the vital costumes to a jumble sale. What else could I do?'

Unsuccessful One-Man Shows

On 7 December 1974, only one man turned up at the 225-seat Centurian Theatre in Carlisle to see David Gooderson's solo performance of *The Castaway*, based on the life of hermit-poet William Cowper. Even so he outnumbered the cast. Mr Gooderson was off with a heavy head cold.

Richard Bright, actor and poet, had the curtain rung down on him after twenty minutes when performing his one-man show at a Drama Festival in Sherringham, Suffolk. Mr Bright couldn't understand why he was stopped before the climax of his performance.

'I have been criticized and abused,' he said, 'and local people have tried to beat me up. I had to run like hell to escape the other night. As soon as I get enough money together I'm off to Cuba. An artist simply isn't appreciated in these parts.

'I was accused of "pawing" women in the audience, but I only went among them to try and wake them up and get some reaction from them. The character I was portraying said it had always been his ambition to make love to a member of the Royal Family – perferably Princess Anne. But that seemed to offend the audience as well. I cannot understand why.'

Mr Bright's main complaint was that he hadn't been allowed to reach the high-spot of his show.

'I would have taken off my mask and clothes and revealed myself in make-up and a pink dress, miming to a Vera Lynn record. I think that's rather good, don't you? At least it's original.'

At the 1983 Edinburgh Festival only one person at a time was admitted to a dank cavern underneath the railway arches to watch Icelandic actor Victor Egg's fifteen-minute show. After the first performance the price of seats (not that there were any) rose from £5 to £25. The organizers, the Circuit Theatre, explained that the rise was necessary to cover the cost of bringing the actor and his backstage team of two to Britain.

Mr Egg's act was a portrayal of an Icelandic monk reciting a confession.

When Orson Welles gave his one-man show of Shakespearean readings in Phoenix, Arizona, only five people turned up.

'Allow me to introduce myself,' said Mr Wells. 'I am an actor, a writer, a director, of both films and plays, an architect, a painter, a stage designer, a brilliant cook, an expert on the corrida, a conjuror, a collector, a connoisseur, an *enfant terrible* and an authority on modern art. How come there are so many of me, and so few of you?' Then he walked off.

Cultural Blackspots

For the Plymouth Theatre Company's production of *The Golden Pathway Annual*, six actors had learned twenty parts between them and the stage-hands took ten hours to erect the scenery. An expensive publicity campaign had blitzed the Devon town of Ashburton with free tickets and a massive distribution of posters.

When the curtain went up at the 200-seat theatre, one man was sitting in the middle of the stalls. At the end of the play, he applauded loudly and left.

But the actors have declared the area a cultural blackspot. The theatre's administrator, Wendy Lost, said: 'Last time we went there with the *Winslow Boy*, nobody turned up at all.'

How come there are so many of me, and so few of you?

Unsuccessful Stage Mothers

In a sensational outburst in New York, Dolly Parton's mother claimed that the busty singing star treats her husband Carl 'worse than a dog'.

Dolly's mother says that the blonde bombshell totally ignores Carl, and even bans him from the main part of their home in Nashville, Tennessee.

She told an American magazine : 'They lead separate lives in the 42-room house. Carl has a bedroom, a small den where he takes his meals, and a bathroom – and Dolly has the rest. I can't recall a single conversation between them in twenty years of marriage.'

Dolly's mother also claimed that while her daughter's biggest assets are real, she wears false teeth.

In 1973 Kathy Kirby was booked for five shows in the course of a cabaret tour of Scotland, but the last three were called off after incidents had marred the first two.

In Dunoon, Argyllshire, two hundred people walked out after the spotlight, worked by Miss Kirby's mother, Mrs Ethel Kirby, consistently failed to pick out the singer.

At the Castle Vaults Club in Kilbirnie, Ayrshire, Miss Kirby reported : 'My mother had mastered the spotlight, but when I had trouble with the microphone she came on stage and shouted, "Stop the show! Stop the show!"'

At a party later there was a disagreement between Mrs Ethel Kirby and a policeman. Mrs Kirby was taken to the police station and appeared in court the next day accused of causing a breach of the peace.

Asked to explain why she had leapt to her feet with a cry of 'Pathetic! Laughable! Get her off!' when her daughter had appeared at a drama school's graduation concert, Mrs Enid Frost, a cleaning lady of Wembley, said, 'I speak as I find.' She explained that every morning for seven years she had got up at five o'clock and, having cooked Mr Frost his breakfast, had bicycled seven miles into central London, where, in spite of a chronically bad back, she scrubbed floors for a living. Mrs Frost had been happy to make this sacrifice to pay the fees at the expensive drama school where her daughter Cheryl was studying.

'Last Saturday was Cheryl's big day,' said Mrs Frost. 'It was the school's annual graduation performance, and Cheryl was appearing in public for the first time. Mr Frost and I were so proud. It was the culmination of all our dreams.'

Asked by a reporter how Cheryl had been, Mrs Frost replied: 'No talent at all. Money down the drain. It's been a hard life, but worth it.'

Unsuccessful Awards

After the British Theatre Association had given out its annual drama awards on 29 January 1981, it was discovered that because of 'computing errors' most of the awards had gone to the wrong people – even though the computer had had to cope with the votes of only six judges.

Judi Dench won the Best Actress Award for her performance in *Juno And The Paycock*, but a count-up after the event showed that she had in fact come a poor second to Frances de la Tour for her work in *Duet For One*.

David de Keyser took home the award for the Best Supporting Actor (*Duet For One*), but the six judges had voted for David Threfall in *Nicholas Nickleby*.

Michael Frayn was surprised to receive the Best New Play Award for *Make Or Break*, since it had been described by the judges as 'a desert, a wasted evening'.

Receiving the Best Musical Award on behalf of the £500,000 flop *Sweeney Todd*, Sheila Hancock said: 'We are the most awarded flop in the history of the theatre. We are expecting an award for that too.'

Apologies were sent and Ion Trewin (Editor of the British Theatre Association's quarterly *Drama*) said that the various *artistes* would be allowed to share the awards 'they either did or did not get'.

Named Entertainer Of The Year in a Variety Club poll, commedian Freddie Starr was due to receive his award at the Lakeside Club, Surrey. It was discovered too late that the club was suing him for £70,000 for failing to turn up for a booking.

Club owner Bob Potter, said: 'Freddie Starr will never set foot in my establishment again.'

Mr Starr was not available for comment. He was in Barbados on doctor's advice.

On 13 February 1979, architects from all over the country assembled on Skegness Pier for the presentation to Mr George Sunderland of the Best Designed Pier Theatre Award.

The Skegness Pier Company now plans to build a new theatre on the beach, to replace the one swept out to sea during the presentation ceremony.

The Least Successful Theatrical Dinner Party

Nicol Williamson was invited to dinner by Kenneth Tynan. He turned up an hour early, catching his hosts unbathed and unchanged. He volunteered to pass the time hoovering the floor. Then he asked, 'Who else is coming?' Tynan told him that one of the guests was Jonathan Miller. 'Biggest phoney in London,' said Williamson crisply. 'Who else?' Tynan told him that there would be a pretty young actress who had been having an affair with Roman Polanski.

When the guests arrived, Williamson aborted polite conversation by producing an LP of the Mamas and Papas and playing it at full volume.

In the dining-room Williamson munched in silence before addressing his first remark to the pretty young actress. Placing his left hand on his right bicep and making a swift upward jab with a clenched right fist, he said, 'So you're the girl who was being fucked by Polanski.'

'Wrong, Mr Williamson,' she said. 'I *am* being fucked by Polanski.'

This exchange seemed to annoy Williamson, and a few minutes later he got up and left the room. There was a deafening five-minute blast of The Mamas and the Papas, then he marched out, slamming the front door.

'I enjoy baboons,' said Dr Miller, 'but preferably in zoos.'

The Least Successful Theatrical Tea Party

Shortly after *Beyond The Fringe* opened in May 1961, Jonathan Miller, Alan Bennett, Peter Cook and Dudley Moore woke up to the fact that while they were each receiving precisely £75 a week for their efforts, the producers – myself and Donald Albery – were trousering a cool £2,000 every pay-day. This didn't seem right, so they wrote a polite letter to the management seeking an adjustment. Mr Albery, whose contribution to the show's success had been to attend the final run-through, after which he had suggested the immediate replacement of 'the one with spectacles' (my own contribution had been even less remarkable), invited them to tea. Over seed cake he explained the economics of the theatre. 'Difficult times ...

rising costs ... rates ... bricks and mortar ... taxes ... review the situation when I get back from the South of France in September ... have another cup of tea.' He then offered them an extra £15 a week each. Out-argued and bowed with remorse, they thanked him humbly for the seed cake and crept away. Mr Albery and I – 'Wish I could help ... hands tied ... over a barrel ... what can I do ?' – continued to share £2,000 a week, until the show went to America, when we did rather better.

Erotic Disasters

'I had no desire to see *The Dirtiest Show In Town* myself, but my wife insisted on it,' said Mr Jim Wedding of Clacton.

After being led away from the Duchess Theatre in a state of shock, Mr Wedding explained that it was not because of anything in the show that he had torn off his trouser leg and stuffed it into the theatre manager's mouth.

'It was a dull show – just as I expected it to be. But during one of the so-called erotic sequences a mouse ran up the leg of my trousers,' he said.

Three Stockholm couples who attended the first night of *Oh ! Calcutta* ! in the nude were surprised when the house manager threw them out.

'We understood you had to be in the nude to get in,' they said.

Millionaire furrier Rodney Parsons made regular visits to a lunchtime sex theatre, believing it to be an orthopaedic clinic.

Mr Parsons, landlord of the members-only Society Theatre Club in Camden, London, pleaded not guilty at Highbury Corner Magistrates Court to being the landlord of premises used as a disorderly house.

'Every time I went to the club the *artistes* covered their

'We understood you had to be in the nude to get in,' they said.

theatrical costumes with white uniforms,' he said, 'and I was massaged by a qualified person. I have been the victim of a confidence trick.'

PC Taylor told the court that after an explicit floor-show he was taken into a cubicle by choreographer Linda Todd and offered champagne and sex services, but he made his excuses.

Miss Todd told the court that she and another dancer called Yvonne had had sex with Parsons. 'It was general knowledge that Parsons would try out the dancers during their first week at the club.'

Parsons, of St John's Wood, denied the charges and was acquitted.

Interpol were alerted after a warrant was issued for the arrest of a run-away grandfather police wanted to interview over the shooting of *Les Deux Sophisticates* in mid-performance.

There were fears that wealthy businessman Nigel Chatsworth, 61, had already left the country. Mr Chatsworth was the former boyfriend of Denise, 22, one of *Les Deux Sophisticates*, who was shot in the behind from a box as she performed on stage at the Tivoli Theatre, Stockton, with her partner Rodney. Police believed that although Mr Chatsworth had left a note at his home he might have fled to the Continent.

On 29 June 1973, a large audience of mothers, delighted to find a pantomime being performed in the middle of the summer, took their children to see *Cinderella* at the Bishop's Park Theatre, Fulham. But at midnight the ballroom became a brothel, Cinderella became a whore, the ugly sisters performed a lesbian *tableau vivant* and the Fairy Godmother acted out a rape scene with Buttons.

Shocked parents have demanded closer control by the council over plays put on at the subsidized Bishop's Park Theatre, but Mrs Chattie Salaman, director of the Commonstock Theatre Company, which mounted the production, said: 'We have performed this show at several London theatres. This is the first time there has been a complaint.'

69

Interviewed after she had been arrested for shop-lifting, Miss Yvonne Bullen, the sex-star, said: 'I just didn't know what I was doing. It's been nothing but work, work, work for the last two years. In over thirty sex shows I have performed more than two thousand erotic acts. You can see that I'm dazed by it all, because the goods for which I forgot to pay were all dog foods for my Alsation, Casanova, and he died two years ago.'

Miss Bullen said that she planned to give up acting to enrol at the Open University.

47-year-old René Gaucher, a former motor mechanic, and his wife Arlette, 35, were arrested at the Theatre des Saints Innocents, Paris, for 'exhibiting the sex act, preceded by obscene gestures and flagellation accompanied by grunts and vulgar comments'.

Gaucher told the court: 'We are legally married and have the right to make love.'

'Not if it offends public morals,' said the judge.

René was quick to spot a flaw in this argument. 'But the public paid to see us do it,' he pointed out, adding: 'We have given seventy performances and each time we did it with real emotion.'

Arlette confided to the judge that she and René lasted the pace because they really loved each other. 'Now we're in show-business,' she said, 'we want a second child and hope it may be conceived on stage before the public.'

René was sent to prison for nine months and Arlette for eighteen, because, said the judge, 'as a woman you should have set a better example.'

In February 1983, Mr David English, a sex show producer of Old Compton Street, Soho, was taken to court by angry customers because his shows were not as explicit as the literature advertising them suggested.

At the hearing, Mr James Godwin of Woking, Surrey, expressed the view that had he been looking merely for unnecessary nudity and simulated copulation he would have stayed at home and watched television.

Mr English was fined £100 by the magistrate and given a twelve-month suspended sentence.

On the last night of *Oh ! Calcutta* ! at The Roundhouse, Chalk Farm, a middle-aged man ran on stage during the nude finale and tried to kiss actor Anthony Booth, 54, live-in lover of *Coronation Street*'s Elsie Tanner.

Retired Guards officer, Major Nigel Godwin, said : 'I have been depressed since leaving the army. The only job I've been offered was serving in a live bait shop. It all got on top of me.'

The Most Disastrous Newspaper Apology

'In last Sunday's *News Of The World*, under the headline "Babsie Goes The Whole Hog For Farmers", we reported that at a strip show our investigators witnessed at the Halifax Conservative Club ruddy-faced farmers in check suits and heavy-soled shoes sipped pints of ale as Barbara "Babsie Blue" Bolton – a 36-year-old blonde – gyrated suggestively between the tables, nuzzling against farmers to the refrain of Vera Lynn's "We'll Meet Again".

'In fact we now discover that the show didn't take place at the Conservative Club, Halifax, but at *Len's Coq Sportif* in Cardiff. Mr Michael Ellison, leader of the Tory-controlled Halifax Borough Council, has pointed out that "Permission would never be given for the Conservative Club premises to be used for such a purpose."

'We apologize for our error.'

Theatre in the Home

Answering a ring at his front door, father of four Bert Long-stuff was surprised to find a gorilla singing 'Happy Birthday To You'. He fetched his shot-gun and peppered the gorilla as it pedalled away on a bicycle. The surprise had been arranged as a birthday treat by Mr Longstuff's four children.

Gorilla-Gram organizer, Mr Harry Meadows, said: 'Mr Longstuff got off lightly. Our speciality is custard pies.'

'My husband takes an interest in music,' said Mrs Wendy Lowe of Ipswich. 'When I saw that Brian Meadway's latest LP included a personal offer from him to perform in the homes of his admirers, I wrote away, giving him the date of our wedding anniversary and our address.

'The doorbell went just after supper and my husband, to whom I had not mentioned the matter, went to answer it. Much to his surprise, Mr Meadway, who was drunk, pushed his way in, said he had been detained at a press conference, and then spent twenty minutes in the lavatory. After this, he joined my husband and my mother (who had come from Torquay for the occasion) and insisted on borrowing my tennis racquet, without which, he said, he couldn't mime the song properly.

'When he began to sing, the neighbours knocked on the wall to stop the noise. Whereupon Mr Meadway pounded back with the racquet and shouted obscenities up the chimney. On the way out he was sick over the hall carpet and when I told him he had spoilt our evening, he said, 'Who cares?''

An early exponent of theatre in the home was Janie Jones, who on Friday evenings in the late sixties entertained Café Society to musical evenings at her house in Camden Hill. Zelda Plum, a twenty-stone army officer's daughter, danced with a parrot on her head, and her manager, Mr Wiley, often took his shoes off and recited all 134 verses of 'Eskimo Nell'. One night the Dirty Squad broke down the front door and ran among the artistes shouting, 'Evening all! We're the Dirty Squad.' Then they planted dildoes in Miss Jones's handbag and arrested her for running a disorderly house. Café Society queued up to give evidence against her and, though she was acquitted, the judge gave her seven years anyway. The Lord Chief Justice reduced this to six on appeal, arguing that seven years was too long for something you hadn't done, but the experimental theatre had suffered another body-blow.

Theatre in a Hotel Room

Caught three-in-a-bed by a security guard in a single room at the Hilton Hotel, Park Lane, Mr Max Irving, a self-alleged impresario with offices in the West End, claimed that he was rehearsing Act III of *The Killing Of Sister George*. The two young ladies, far from being masseuses from an agency, were Equity members, said Mr Irving, keen to further their careers. One was playing the Susannah York role, said Mr Irving, the other Coral Browne's, while he himself was appearing, and not for the first time, as Beryl Reid. An Equity representative was called, who confirmed that the two young ladies were indeed on Equity's books, but that, since simulated sex was about to take place, an Equity observer must be present, as per Equity Resolution 652. He sat down and called for room service, whereupon Mr Irving postponed the show.

Theatre in the Street

In the summer of 1982, Instant Madness, a group of London-based street performers, went to Newcastle to take part in the North-East Arts Festival of Music and Drama. They ate fire,

He sat down and called for room service, whereupon Mr Irving postponed the show.

lay on nails and walked around in their underwear with poles on their heads. Tim Robinson, from Battersea, the group leader, set fire to his beard with a fire-stick, Jackie Jones, the leading lady, broke both wrists while doing a handstand, Des Withers was bitten by an Alsatian and Ronnie Lane, dressed as a circus *auguste*, was knocked down by the driver of a Ford Fiesta, who drove on and then, feeling remorse, no doubt, came back and knocked him down again.

'There hasn't been much to laugh about on Tyneside recently,' said Festival organizer Bill Parry, 'so we've invited them back next year.'

Theatre by the Docks

Robert Atkins was walking by Bristol docks with a fellow actor when he stopped by a magnificent four-masted schooner.

'Look at that beautiful barque !' he cried. 'She has sailed the seven seas to bring us tea from Ceylon, jewels from India, silks from China, spices from Samarkand, and there she lies about to depart at our behest.' He called to a deckhand, bent over a hawser. 'Sailor! Whither sailest thou?'

'Fuck off,' said the deckhand, without looking up.

Theatre on the Water

Mikron, a theatre group of the inland waterways, moored their barge at Berkhamstead, Bucks, and performed a documentary on the history of the canals called *Still Waters*. After the show, theatre director Mr Fred Dunne and his wife, Nora, stepped out of the stage door and fell into the canal.

Following them out of the stage door were fellow members

of the company, Noel Dooley and his girlfriend Cindy Fairfax. As soon as Fred and Nora Dunne hit the water, Noel and Cindy dived in to rescue them.

Unfortunately, none of them could swim. Two more members of the group, John Wallace and Tony Hampton, hearing the four crying for help, dived in too. Alas, they too were non-swimmers.

By this time a large crowd had gathered at the canal's edge. Shouts of encouragement and blame were directed at the drowning six, and at last two policemen, alerted by the noise, came on the scene. They immediately dived in, but, like the other six, turned out to be non-swimmers.

Two passers-by, Mr Jack Chambers and Mr Harry Fieldhouse, then jumped in. They were strong swimmers but were soon pulled under by their rescuees and in no time were drowning too. Twenty feet above them the crowd had grown larger. A man appeared with a loud-hailer to give advice; a woman seized it from him and reminded the drowners of the evils of their theatrical pasts and alcoholic ways.

At last the fire brigade arrived. It took them fifteen minutes to force their way through the crowd and to the water's edge. They pulled the ten from the water and only the two strong swimmers, Mr Chambers and Mr Fieldhouse, were seriously hurt. The ambulance took them to hospital. The other eight, including the two policemen, became involved in a long argument with the crowd.

The Least Successful Lunchtime Theatre

Attired in bowler hats, silk capes, jeans and, in one case, a leopard-skin bikini, The Survivors Theatre Group were performing a 'Women's Basic Human Right To Take Responsibility For Their Own Bodies' revue at the Little Theatre Club, St Martin's Lane, when the bailiffs burst in and padlocked the doors.

'This is Rachmanism,' said group leader Jan Shipton. 'Just what we'd expect from capitalist landlords. But why should the audience suffer?'

It was pointed out to her that there hadn't been an audience.

Old Bill Takes a Hand

Old actors share with MPs the need to expose themselves after hours on street corners. A resourceful defence to the charge was put forward by Mr Brian Dicey, a member of the Royal Shakespeare Company, arrested for indecent exposure in the middle of Lenin Square, Kiev.

'I have never seen such a delighted audience as packed the theatre on Monday night to see *Hamlet*,' said Mr Dicey. 'Walking about the city the next day was a real eye-opener. People rushed up and offered to buy my clothes for fantastic sums. My tie went for a fiver. I got forty-five pounds for my jacket and thirty for my trousers. Before I knew what was happening I was down to my socks.'

Mr Dicey told the police that the man to whom he had sold his trousers had assured him that he could buy another pair just round the corner at a quarter of the price.

'But when I got there,' said Mr Dicey, 'the shop was closed.'

As part of their Theatre Of The Absurd season, the Prakomachaii District Mime Company were rehearsing a scene from Eugene Ionesco's *Rhinoceros* when police burst on to the stage and shot dead Mr Dam Saeng Dung, the company's leading actor.

A fellow actor, Mr Vichien Benjawan, was the alleged thief of Mr Dung's wig.

'We have apologized to Mr Dung's family,' said a police

My tie went for a fiver.

spokesman. 'When Mr Dung informed us of his rendez-vous with the notorious thief, Benjawan, he unfortunately enclosed a ten-by-eight photograph of himself rather than of the criminal.'

'If that isn't absurd, you tell me what is,' Mr Dung's widow said to reporters.

On 18 August 1953, during a performance of *The Office Is Empty* in a mountain village in Catalan, a squad of Guardia Civil stood up in the audience and shot dead three members of Los Joglers theatre troupe. They claimed that the play insulted General Franco and the armed forces, and libelled the police, dubbing them as brutal.

A performance of *Snow White And The Seven Dwarfs* at the Shaftesbury Theatre was interrupted in 1983 when members of the Robbery Squad ran on-stage and arrested a professional wrestler, Mr Raymond McCray, in connection with a £45,000 bank hold-up at Ilford.

Mr McCray, a three-and-a-half-foot dwarf, had been able to avoid surveillance cameras because his head had remained below the counter during the tickle.

Arriving for work one morning in 1962, executives of MCA, the vast world-wide talent agency, found FBI officers sitting at their desks, answering their phones, dictating letters and doing deals. The agency wing of MCA had been closed down by the government under the new monopoly laws.

In their first week in charge, FBI agents booked the National Theatre into a tent in Idaho, Frank Sinatra into Max's Fish Restaurant, Moosejaw, at sixty dollars a night and bought the film rights to *Gone With The Wind* for $15,000. They also advised Howard Duff to look for a new agent.

Mr X, a successful impresario, but with the appearance and address of a carpet-bagger, arrived one morning at his luxurious Mount Street offices to discover a little man in a mask and striped jumper, and with a sack marked 'Swag', struggling out of the front door with his television set and video recorder. Mr X collared him and called the police.

The police listened to both sides of the story and, deciding that Mr X was an obvious fantasist, let the masked thief go.

That might have been the end of the matter, had not the thief, later in the day, tried the same trick at other premises. This time he was arrested and, with the new evidence, was also charged with the theft of Mr X's equipment.

Eight weeks later the matter came to court. It seemed an open and shut case. The thief, after all, had been caught red-handed, with a jemmy under his striped jersey, a set of skeleton keys and a sack marked 'Swag'. Then Mr X was called to give evidence. The jury, like the arresting officers originally, found him so obviously lacking in credibility that they immediately acquitted the thief.

Actress Helen Slater, whose career took off the day she was picked to play Supergirl, revealed her secret dream exclusively to the *Daily Mail*.

'I'd rather be a clown,' she said, and in no time at all she'd tucked her hair into a funny hat, put on a red nose and set off for Hyde Park in pixie boots.

Disgusted Royal Parks police officers immediately arrested her for suspicious behaviour.

Disastrous First Nights

Moss Hart's first play, *The Beloved Bandit*, rejected by seventeen managements, was at last put on by Augustus Pitou Jr – 'King of the One-Night Stands'. Hart's elation knew no bounds, but at the opening in Chicago nothing went right. The curtain jammed as the lights dimmed, and the set, of a bilious green colour which Hart had never seen duplicated, buckled during the first five minutes, stunning the character man. There was a lengthy wait while it was secured, and when the star, a 6 ft 4ins Irishman called Joseph Regan, entered singing a ballad he tripped over a stage brace and fell smack into the fireplace. As he picked himself up, cursing, the rain, which had been bucketing down all day, turned into hail the size of marbles and hit the theatre's roof so insistently that for the next twenty minutes not a word of dialogue could be heard. 'A small mercy,' wrote Hart, 'for which I was not at the time sufficiently grateful.'

Nothing worked. If an actor went to open a door it either stuck or came clean away in his hand. At one point, when the leading lady opened a window to call after Regan, it came off the frame and she was left holding it centre-stage. By the second act, the actors dithered hopelessly about the stage, waiting for the next calamity. It came soon enough. Joseph Regan, the giant Irishman, making his second-act entrance through the same door, tripped over the same stage brace – only this time the fireplace collapsed under his enormous weight. The audience sat through the second and third acts in grim silence – even when Regan, for reasons of his own, made his third-act entrance *through* the fireplace with a line composed by himself, and never explained: 'Every day's Christmas when the Irish come to town,' he announced cheerfully.

As the final curtain fell, a mass exodus started, as though, Hart wrote later, twenty-dollar gold pieces were being distributed free in the street outside. There was not even a smattering of applause. Actors bowed to a solid phalanx of retreating backs. Moss Hart went backstage and met the stage manager – cheerful for the first time since rehearsals began.

'Never saw one go worse,' he said, smiling. 'I've seen them going all kinds of ways, but that was like spraying ether. I wouldn't wait up for the critics if I were you. I know one of the critics here, and he waits all year for one to come along like this.'

In 1979, anglophile Wally Paterson, New Zealand's leading impresario, imported Norman Wisdom to top the bill in *Wally Paterson's London Follies* at the Regency Theatre, Auckland. On the first night he sat proudly in a box in a teddy-bear overcoat and polished pumps, but, alas, he'd made many mistakes. His first had been to open with the seals. They were a good turn (possibly the best on the bill, not excluding the monkeys due to come on before Norman), but their slippery antics left the stage like an ice-rink. Next on were the girls, who skated straight into the stalls. They recovered, but were soon in trouble again when the dance captain's bra broke. She alone knew the steps, so when she retired to get a safety-pin, the others, who had been following her, all danced into each other and ended on the floor. Next on was the *ingénue*, who went into the stalls with hand-held mike, singing 'Let Me Entertain You'. The spotlight following her broke, leaving her stumbling round in the dark, still singing as she searched for the exit. She'd have still been crashing around at the interval, had not the next turn brought the show to a halt. Demetrius and Cheryl, contortionists and acrobats – he dressed as a Roman gladiator, she as a slave-girl – were doing well until an unusual acrobatic move left those in the front stalls in no doubt that Cheryl had left her knickers in the dressing-room. While she was off repairing this oversight, Demetrius blew up hot-water bottles until one exploded in his face, hurling him twenty feet backwards into the set, a permanent flat depicting Piccadilly Circus, knocking it over and so startling Vera 'Eros' Blaine, posing on a pedestal, that she shot a plywood arrow into the bottom of Denise 'Moon Goddess' Vane, who was posing nearby in the nude. Words were exchanged between the two, Demetrius was taken to hospital and the curtain was brought down. The theatre never reopened, but shortly afterwards became New Zealand's first gay disco – until burned down after two nights by enraged locals.

The Least Successful Prompt

When Alan Ayckbourn's *How The Other Half Loves* went on tour in America, Phil Silvers took over the role played by Robert Morley in London. Arriving in America shortly before the opening, Ayckbourn was appalled to discover that Silvers, apart from being the greatest comedian in the world and a very nice man, had completely lost his memory. He knew none of his lines, but by the time they opened in Palm Springs, Gene Saks, the director, by working feverishly with Silvers, had got him more or less familiar with Acts I and II. Of the third act he knew not a word. They decided to rely on a prompter, but Saks and Ayckbourn were worried when they got to Palm Springs because they saw at once that the stage didn't allow for one. Like many American stages it was enormously wide. There was nowhere a prompter could sit without a loud-hailer because the prompt-corner was a football field's length from the centre of the stage.

'We'll cut a hole in the forestage,' said Saks.

'You can't,' said the carpenter. 'It's aluminium.'

'I don't care about the cost,' said Saks. 'We're having a trap, like an opera box, in the front of the stage.'

So, amid great protests, they cut a hole, and into the hole went Tom Erhardt, the assistant director, who'd been helping Silvers with his lines. Erhardt was bald, and when they put the lights on, his head shone like a moon in the middle of the stage. So they darkened his head with a black beret, which made him look like a Provisional IRA man crouching in a slit trench.

Palm Beach has the reputation of being the worst place in the world. The audience is made up of wizened socialites, all of whom leave after the interval. They never see the second half – their chauffeurs have been ordered for after the interval. They'd have their champagne, be photographed and leave. So there was Erhardt in his hole with the book, and Silvers was going great guns, and the play was so good that quite a few chauffeurs were told to wait after the interval. The manager was ecstatic. No third act had ever had an audience before. The curtain closed for a change before the last scene, but was so thin that the entire house heard Silvers shouting to Erhardt in the hole, 'I need you now, baby !'

The curtain parted and Silvers started the last scene. Erhardt wasn't a professional prompter. There is a great art, apparently, to giving the key word quickly and clearly. Erhardt had a loud voice, but was very slow. Soon Silvers dried completely.

'Well, Bob, I think ... I think ... I think ... where are you, Tom?'

'Possibly,' said Erhardt.

Silvers had a buzzing in the ears and couldn't hear him. 'Well, Bob, I think ... I think ... I think ...'

'Possibly,' shouted a man at the back of the stalls.

Silvers was inconsolable at having been prompted by a member of the audience.

First-Night Nerves

Engaged by Sir Donald Wolfit for a provincial tour, a novice actor was overwhelmed by stage fright on the opening night in Oxford. He came on and was immediately at a loss for words. All he could remember was that his character had little respect for the hero. So he spat in Sir Donald's face and swaggered off.

For a production of *Antony And Cleopatra* at the Piccadilly Theatre in 1946, a very inexperienced young actor was engaged to play the part of Eros, whose only function was to assist in removing Antony's armour.

'Unarm me, Eros,' said Godfrey Tearle as Antony, 'the long day's task is done. Off, pluck off.'

The shaking actor was mortified. 'I'm so sorry, Mr Tearle,' he said, and ran off the stage.

Appearing with Robert Atkins at the Open Air Theatre, Regent's Park, a young actor was supposed to come on as a page at the start of the play with the line: 'My Lord, the King is here.' Nervous on the first night, he entered and delivered the line : 'My Lord, the King is dead.'

Robert Atkins took him by the throat and shook him like a rat. 'The words by the greatest poet the world has ever known,' he bellowed. 'The scenery, by God! The director a genius, though I say so myself. And YOU come on and bugger the whole play up.'

The Worst Orchestra

In 1943 Peter Ustinov was sent to Salisbury where he directed *The Rivals* with Edith Evans as Mrs Malaprop. 'We had a happy mixture of civilian and military actors,' writes Ustinov, 'and, as an unexpected bonus, eight members of the Berlin Philharmonic Orchestra, under their leader, Lance-Corporal Professor Doktor Reinhard Strietzel, and seven members of the Vienna Philharmonic, under their leader Private Professor Doctor Rudolf Stiasny, all now members of the Pioneer Corps, a section of the British army organised as a reserve of foreign talent, eager to do their bit against Hitler.

'Rehearsals had their ups and downs. The orchestra seemed divided against itself, the first violin and conductor, Professor Strietzel, seeming to be at loggerheads with the first cello, Professor Stiasny, which culminated in an ugly scene, during which Lance-Corporal Strietzel threatened to put Professor Stiasny under close arrest. He pointed to the single stripe on his arm with the tip of his bow, calling out in a thick German accent, "You know vat zis means ?"

'The conflict was complicated by the intervention of Edith

Evans, who reminded us all that it was a play with music, not an opera with dialogue. Immediately the musical contention between Austria and the Reich was forgotten. All fifteen bickering musicians were united against Edith Evans. As they filed out of the rehearsal hall to make way for the mummers, Professor Strietzel looked at poor Edith and said, "I don't know . . . how all zis . . . shall end!"

'One drawback of those garrison theatres was that there was no method of concealing the orchestra. Its members sat on the same level as the audience. It was merely the actors who were elevated. I noticed on the first night that the orchestra made use of a miniature chessboard in order to while away the time during the histrionics, and often musicians crept forward like troops in a dugout to make a move. As far as I could understand it, it was a permanent championship, Berlin versus Vienna.

'I hoped and prayed that Edith Evans wouldn't notice what was going on, but on the fourth night, during a brilliant tirade, she stopped dead. One eye had alighted on the tiny chessboard just as an Austrian viola player had spotted a crack in the enemy defence, and was creeping forward to deliver the *coup de grâce*.

'She was livid, and after the show I accosted Professor Strietzel. To soften the blow somewhat I told him he had never played better than on that night.

'His face lit up. "You are a *real* musician," he counter-flattered.

'"There's only one thing . . . one criticism."

'"Ach!" His face darkened.

'"The game of chess. It's frightfully distracting."

'"It *distracts* you?"

'"Yes."

'"No!" he roared. "You are too fine an artist to be distracted. It's zis voman!"

'The next night Edith found it hard to concentrate, which was quite unlike her. As soon as I came on-stage I saw what was happening. The orchestra, deprived of its chessboard, had

86

now arranged the lights on its music-stands so that its members were lit from beneath, and they all followed Edith's every move in this ghostly light, looking like war criminals following the arguments of their advocate with misgiving and resignation.

'Once again, at the end of the performance, I was compelled to accost Professor Strietzel. "I have a criticism."

'"Please?"

'"Why do you follow Edith Evans with your eyes in a manner calculated to disturb any performer, any artist?

'"First it vas the chessboard. Correct me if I am wrong. Chess ve shouldn't play...."

'"That is correct."

'"So ve leave the chessboard at home. Vot else can ve do? Ve follow the play. Ve look at the voman."

'Suddenly the constriction of his voice and the coolness of presentation of the facts deserted him. He shouted volcanically, "You think it gives us *pleasure* to vatch zis voman? Ve who have seen Paula Wessely at her height?"

'The next night Edith was brilliant. The only trouble was the entire absence of laughs. I made my entrance, and, inspired by the zest and brio of Edith, I acted as well as I knew how, in complete and utter silence. It was acutely depressing. Not even the presence of three generals in the front row could justify the extraordinary dullness of the audience.

'When I had a free moment, I rushed to the back of the auditorium to unravel the mystery. I did not have far to seek. The musicians had now reversed their positions, and sat facing the audience, their heads just visible above the rail of the orchestra pit. Lit from beneath, like mournful skittles waiting for the usual knocks of fate, they had utterly dampened the spirits of the onlookers.'

The Worst Dressing-Room

Robert Helpmann was touring America in the ballet, *A Mid-summer Night's Dream*. In one town there was no suitable theatre, so they performed in a floodlit sports arena.

Helpmann was allocated the umpire's changing-room, since they thought the star should have the best accommodation. When the stage manager called the half, he got no answer from the umpire's changing-room, so he opened the door to check that everything was all right. He found Helpmann standing precariously on a chair, which was itself standing on a table, craning his face towards the solitary light-bulb dangling from the ceiling, putting on his elaborate green and gold eye make-up for his part as the king of the fairies.

'Are you all right?' asked the stage manager in alarm.

Helpmann looked down and said, 'Oh yes, I'm fine. But heaven knows how these umpires manage.'

The Worst Stage Door Keeper

The stage door keeper at the Haymarket Theatre was a silly old fool called Bibby, who was much loved in the profession in spite of being quite hopeless at taking and passing on messages.

During the late forties and early fifties, the stage manager at the Haymarket, Charles La Trobe, used to organize all the theatrical memorial services, together with George Bishop, theatre correspondent of the *Daily Telegraph*. These tradition-ally took place at St Paul's, Covent Garden, or St Martin-in-the-Fields. When Bishop left a message for La Trobe at the Haymarket concerning the final arrangements for James Agate's memorial service, it reached La Trobe as: 'Mr A. Gate will be at Sir Martin Field's at 11.30 and would like you to join him.'

When Sam Wanamaker left a message at the Haymarket for Sir John Gielgud, it reached Sir John as : 'Sam wants to make you.'

Bibby could be impatient with time-wasters. When a first night at the Haymarket dragged interminably due to a series of mishaps, Bibby walked on-stage, handed the stage-door keys to the leading man and instructed him to lock up, because he was going home.

The Least Successful Theatrical Creditor

In March 1984, run-away impresario Max Irving spoke to *The Sun* about his amazing romance with the girl he stole from one of his creditors.

Irving, 48, fled to Spain when his touring version of *Ladies Night In A Turkish Bath*, mounted with a stolen American Express card, flopped disastrously, leaving debts of £187,000.

The managing director of the firm from whom Irving hired the costumes, Vic Farrer (Theatrical Costumiers) Ltd, sent his wife Gail, 36, to Spain claiming the £25,000 he said Irving owed him. But by the time Mr Farrer flew to Spain himself a week later, Gail had set up home with Mr Irving.

Speaking from his villa on the Costa Brava, Irving told a *Sun* reporter : 'I had known Gail in England, and when she suddenly arrived here things just clicked.'

Mr Farrer said bitterly : 'I failed to get my money, and now he's got Gail too.'

'Oh yes, I'm fine. But heaven knows how these umpires manage.'

The Least Successful PR Stunts

On 15 April 1975, Cal Cavendish, the country and western singer, was charged by the Royal Canadian Mounted Police with dropping a manure-bomb on a local golf club in Edmonton.

'He buzzed the club-house a couple of times,' said Captain Henry, 'and on his third run threw two carrier-bags filled with horse-shit over the members and their friends.'

Cavendish explained : 'All publicity is good publicity. I had a concert two nights later and intended to leave nothing to chance.'

A similar mishap occurred in 1982 when the citizens of Medicine Bowl, Arizona, found themselves one Thanksgiving Morning being bombed by a hundred turkeys in Yankee-Doodle-Dandy hats thrown from a low-flying aircraft by the publicity manager of the local radio station. There were no fatalities among the locals, but those turkeys that survived the drop were killed instantly as they hit the streets. The publicity manager had assumed turkeys could fly.

The Worst Report from Drama School

Peter Ustinov's final report from drama school stated : 'He has a long way to go. He is still lamentably stiff. He seems to have great difficulty in walking, or running, or jumping. His mind wanders during gymnastics. His voice is unresonant and monotonous.'

His father read the report with alarm. 'At your age,' he said, 'I was as supple as a willow. I jumped, I ran, and walked most outstandingly, my mind never wandered during gymnastics, my voice was powerful and sparkling with colour. Nothing will come of you. Nothing.'

. . . handed the stage-door keys to the leading man . . .

The Worst Othello

In June 1972, British director and playwright Donald Howarth produced *Othello* in South Africa. When he was told that he couldn't have a black man in an otherwise all-white cast, he left out the character of Othello and created three new characters to fill the gap. He claimed that in spite of the reconstruction the play did not differ drastically from Shakespeare's version.

Censorship

Successive Lord Chamberlains banned works by Shelley, Ibsen, Wilde, Shaw, Arthur Miller and John Osborne. Many playwrights treasure letters from the Lord Chamberlain's office suggesting small improvements in their work. When he submitted *The Entertainer*, John Osborne was advised to omit 'rogered', 'shagged', 'turds', 'balls' and 'had', and to change 'the vicar's got the clappers' to 'the vicar's dropped a clanger'. In *The World Of Paul Slickey* there were objections to 'fairy', 'queer' and 'crumpet', the suggested alternatives being 'swishy', 'peculiar' and 'muffin'.

Charles Wood has a letter advising that 'wherever the word "shit" appears "it" would be an improvement'. He was also asked not to use the expression 'I'll have your cobblers' in *Meals On Wheels*. He was seriously perturbed by the suggested substitution : the mysterious and sinister phrase 'I'll have your ollies'.

I regretted the end of censorship. Trying to outflank the censor was one of the few pleasures in theatrical management, and when he went it was, as Robert Frost said of writing free verse, like playing tennis without a net. Taking tea with Colonel Penn of the Lord Chamberlain's office was always a delight, and since he was obviously far too sensible a man ever to go to the theatre, I never paid any attention to his cuts. How was he going to know whether they'd been effected? Two shows did present difficulties because neither had a script: *The Premise* (which was improvised) and *Nights at the Comedy* (a series of music-hall turns). I was rather proud of my solution to the problems these raised. I submitted two innocuous comedies kept on file for just this purpose, having altered their title pages to *The Premise* and *Nights at the Comedy*. The uncensored shows were performed without a murmur of protest from Colonel Penn. Why other managers took any notice of him was always a mystery to me.

The Worst Theatrical Digs

'I did it!' admitted Miss Ida Rubell, the theatrical landlady, during her trial in September 1979 for abducting, killing, plucking and cooking a performing parrot called Arthur, before serving it with rice as the dish of the day.

'Arthur was no ordinary performer,' said his owner, George 'Parrots are my Business' Birch, who had been staying at Miss Rubell's guest-house in Leeds. 'He spoke three languages, ate scrambled eggs, and had a small but varied repertoire of nineteenth-century love songs.'

'Mr Birch was an excellent guest,' said Miss Rubell, 'but I couldn't take the parrot. It waddled round the hall asking for its bill and complaining about the service. It was me or the parrot.'

Miss Rubell was bound over to keep the peace.

The publicity manager had assumed turkeys could fly.

Unsuccessful Auditions

Noël Coward gave Kenneth More a copy of his new play *Peace In Our Time* and invited him to dinner in his flat a few days later. They were alone, Coward in a polka-dot dress. Noël sat down at the piano after dinner and played. The atmosphere was intimate – subdued lighting, seductive music, the fire burning low. Kenneth More sat by the fire with his legs locked together, but lost his nerve when Coward put on a Judy Garland record. He leapt to his feet.

'Oh Mr Coward, sir! I could *never* have an affair with you, because ... because ... you remind me of my mother.'

Council rent collector Arthur Stainrod resigned after housewives in Plymouth claimed that in the course of his rounds he said he was auditioning for a local production of *The Pirates Of Penzance* and invited tenants to remove their clothes.

'I removed my woolly and he touched me,' said housewife Lesley Chown. 'He said he'd let me know.'

An inquiry into the allegations was dropped, but Mr Stainrod resigned in order to 'hang on to my self-respect'.

'I had no alternative,' added the 48-year-old father of two. 'There's no way I'd have come out of this in a good light. Some of the mud would have stuck.'

Unsuccessful Stage-Door Johnnies

To get into the right mood when playing Shylock in *The Merchant Of Venice*, Edmund Kean used to beat up an old actor kept on the pay-roll solely for this purpose. One night the old actor was off injured, so Kean told the stage manager to find him another. Moments later, an ardent admirer of Kean's turned up at the stage door, having travelled all the way from Cornwall to see his hero. The stage door keeper sent him to

. . . before serving it with rice as the dish of the day.

Kean's dressing-room, where Kean, supposing him to be the substitute punch-bag, beat him up.

Leaving the Victoria Palace stage door after a performance of *Hi-Di-Hi*, Simon Callow was surprised when a fan said that unless he gave him his autograph and fifty pence for a cup of coffee he'd hit him with a piece of concrete. Mr Callow refused, so the fan hit him with the concrete. Mr Callow was taken to hospital and the fan to West End Central.

The Least Successful Attempt to Raise Money

When Fenella Fielding's *So Much To Remember* was a hit at The Establishment in 1963, Nicholas Luard and I decided to transfer it to a West End theatre. We booked the Vaudeville, and I raised my half of the capital from the new owner of the Establishment, Raymond Nash, with whom I had recently palled up. He was able, with a sudden upward flick of two fingers, to take the nose clean off a person's face and, as a precautionary measure, employed a bodyguard whose speciality was biting people's ears off. Had Nash not been caught smuggling gold he would undoubtedly have taken over the West End's protection rackets, run at that time by senior officers of the Vice Squad. Deciding to take the weight off his feet, he sat down at Tokyo airport, whereupon the chair collapsed under the weight of gold he had concealed about his person.

Nicholas Luard raised his share of the money from Michael 'Dandy Kim' Waterfield (where Dandy Kim had got it is anybody's guess). When Nash heard this, he arrived in my office in a tremendous state of indignation, tore up his investor's agreement and scattered it on the floor. He couldn't afford, he said, to have his name associated with someone of Dandy Kim's *louche* reputation. We opened at the Vaudeville without my share of the capital, a shortfall from which I never altogether recovered.

The Least Successful Attempt To Influence a Critic

At the first night of *The Secretary Bird*, William Douglas-Home and his wife sat in stall seats on the aisle. As the lights dimmed, he left his seat to calm his nerves by pacing up and down outside. Just before the curtain rose, a figure tip-toed through the darkness and took Douglas-Home's seat. His wife, thinking he'd returned, took his hand at intervals throughout the act to soothe his nerves and patted his knee reassuringly. She was surprised when she eventually received a clout over the head with a handbag. Sitting next to her was Jack Tinker, theatre critic of the *Daily Mail*.

The Least Successful Theatrical Investment

Rubbish-tip worker Philip Collins's dream was to become a West End Angel. For ten years he saved every penny he could, putting nearly all his earnings into a building society account while working as a sweeper at a garbage dump, and then lost the lot – £15,000 – in the £500,000 flop musical *Jeeves*.

'For ten years I lived the life of a monk,' said Philip, 29, who is now living with his parents and hopes to get a job in his father's waste skip firm.

The Most Unsuccessful Attempt
to Keep a Play Running

When J. P. Donleavy's *Fairy Tales Of New York* opened at the Comedy Theatre in 1961, the reviews were good and business at first was brisk. Approaching Easter, however, audiences fell away and there seemed a danger that the box-office receipts would drop below the figure at which the theatre's proprietor, Sir Donald Albery, could give the play notice. The producers were a couple of wallies – myself and Lord Dynevor, to be precise – and thought that if the play could survive this bumpy patch it would run cheerfully throughout the tourist season. We decided, therefore, to boost the weekly receipts above the danger figure by injecting some £2,000 into the box-office ourselves – a practice specifically forbidden in the contract with Sir Donald Albery, which, as is customary, referred to the *bona fide* sale of seats to the public.

Buying seats for your own show is not as easy as it might seem. You can't just hop down to the theatre with £2,000 in used notes and ask for five hundred stalls. The tickets have to be bought in dribs and drabs by apparently genuine theatregoers. Lord Dynevor took £2,000 out of the bank and gave it to Bert Leywood, the general manager I'd inherited from Jack Waller. The silly old fool tottered off to the Berwick Street fruit market, where he was well known, and distributed it like confetti among the surprised barrow-boys with the instruction that they should go immediately to the Comedy Theatre and buy front stalls for J. P. Donleavy's wry, elusive work. Most thought Christmas had come early, but an honourable minority did as they were told. A sudden queue of fruiterers at the Comedy's box-office alerted Donald Albery to irregular goings-on, and he posted his gimlet-eyed son Ian in the foyer to stop the monkey-business.

It was our misfortune that no sooner had young Albery taken up his position than thirty vicars arrived at the box-office, wanting seats for that night. Young Albery, assuming

She was surprised when she eventually received a clout over the head with a handbag.

they were extras hired by Lord Dynevor and myself, sent them packing, having, to their surprise, first attempted to tear their dog-collars off. The party of vicars was all the proof Donald Albery needed that we were buying seats. I was summoned and given a rocket, while J.P.Donleavy, who had no idea what Lord Dynevor and I were up to, went to the box-office and tried to buy six seats for friends later in the week. Young Albery, still on guard, stepped forward and accused him of conspiracy in the plot. Donleavy, not a man falsely to accuse of anything, was so inai̯ɔ nant that he king-punched young Albery, laying him out as flat as a pancake on the floor of his own theatre.

The Albery family had the last laugh, however. Hardly any of Lord Dynevor's £2,000 found its way into the box-office, the receipts fell below the safety figure, and the play was given notice.

The Most Disastrous Use of the Word 'Inimitable' in a Book of Theatrical Anecdotes

Gyles Brandreth writes : 'That reminds me of the occasion when the stills photographer was on-stage at a dress rehearsal for a Broadway revue, taking pictures of the two leading ladies, one of whom was Beatrice Lillie.

' "Could you step back a little further, ladies ?" asked the young photographer.

' "Why ?" snapped La Lillie (sic).

' "Because he wants us in focus," explained her co-star.

' "What – both of us ?" retorted the inimitable Miss Lillie.'

. . . thirty vicars arrived at the box-office . . .

The Most Unsuccessful Anecdote in a Theatrical Memoir by Peter Ustinov

When Rector of Dundee University, Peter Ustinov received a letter addressed to 'The Lord Rectum of Dundee University'. 'And that is how I have seen myself ever since in moments of self-doubt.'

The Most Unsuccessful Anecdote in a Theatrical Memoir Not by Peter Ustinov, but involving Noël Coward

Derek Salberg writes: 'I served on several Arts Council Drama Panels, along with a number of famous actors. At a meeting Noël Coward attended, the future of the Old Vic was discussed and a representative of that theatre made an impassioned plea for better seats in the gallery where, he said, "school-children had to sit on hard wooden seats".

'"Serve them right – little beasts," said Coward.'

The Most Unsuccessful Riposte Involving Noël Coward in a Theatrical Memoir

Joyce Grenfell writes: 'When *Cat On A Hot Tin Roof* opened on Broadway in 1964, Noël Coward wagged a finger at me and said that I *must* go and see it. I was playing eight performances a week at the time, and though I could have managed a matinée I didn't feel much call to see the play.

'"You *should* go," said Noël. "Such things go on in real life."

'"So does diarrhoea," I riposted, "but I don't fancy paying a lot of dollars to go and watch it."'

The Most Unsuccessful Reference to the Outbreak of War in a Theatrical Memoir

Peter Ustinov writes: 'In 1939 I was offered the understudy of George Devine, which was not bad going for a Shakespearean clown at the start of his career. I accepted and made plans to leave home at the first pay-day. Unfortunately, that master of the dramatic, Adolf Hitler, opened before we even had a chance to go into rehearsal, and with him as impresario, I slowly prepared to play a part I was totally unsuited to, for the worst pay, in a run lasting over four years.'

The Least Successful Use of the Word 'Chinese' in a Book of Theatrical Anecdotes

Gyles Brandreth writes: 'In 1964 Marti Stevens was playing Elvira in *High Spirits*, the musical version of Noël Coward's *Blithe Spirit*. Following her opening line – "Good evening, Charles" – spoken through a microphone, she was supposed to fly off the stage on a wire. The microphone had a short circuit, and as she said her line, an electric shock knocked her off her platform, leaving her to swing from side to side, before she was dumped ignominiously on her rear end in the centre of the stage. Coward went backstage during the interval and quipped inimitably:

'"I'm very proud of you, darling. You managed to play the first act of my little comedy tonight with all the Chinese flair and light-hearted brilliance of Lady Macbeth."'

Index